3-Minut
Motivators

3-Minute Motivators

More than 100 activities to help you REACH, TEACH and ACHIEVE

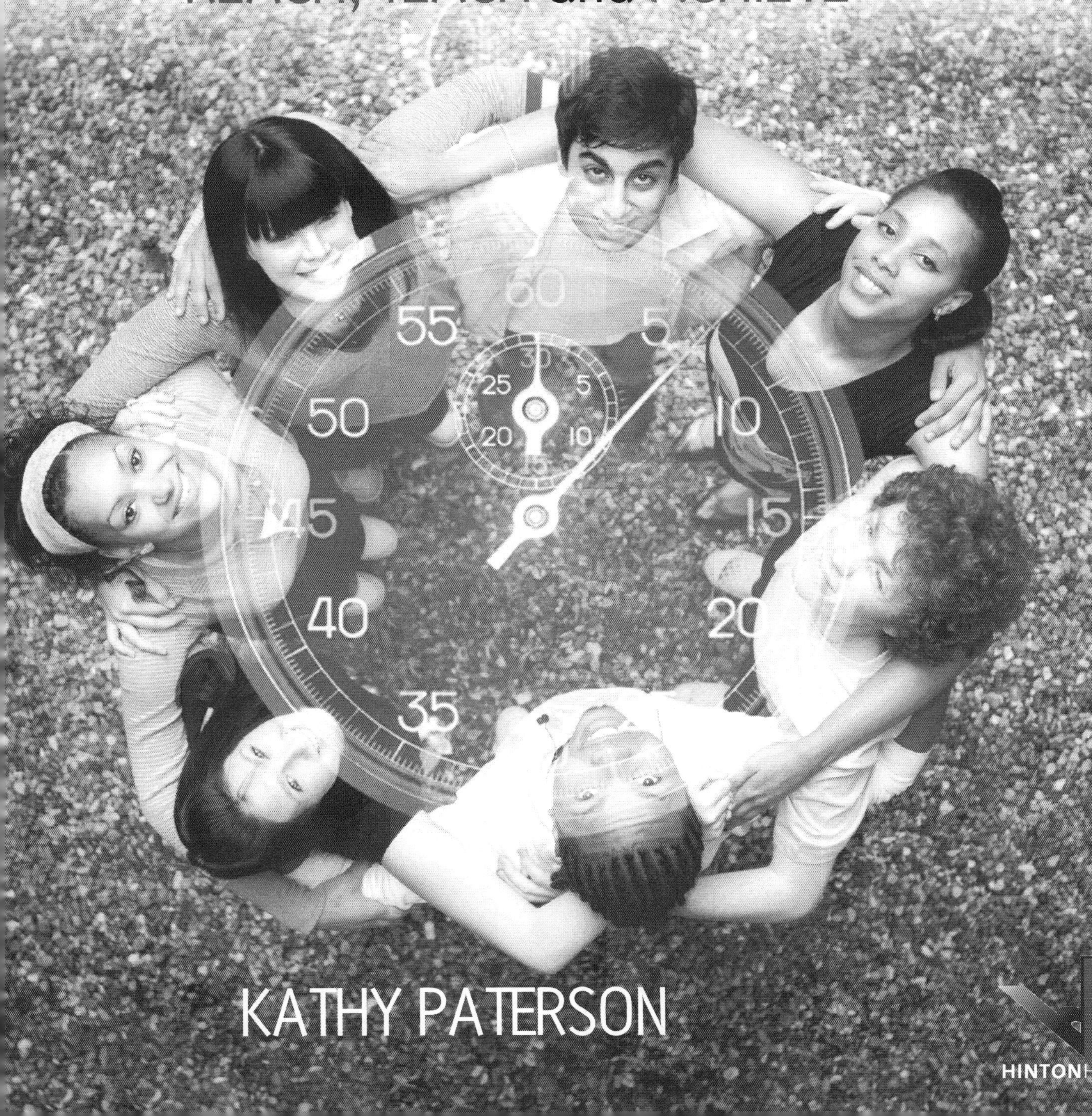

KATHY PATERSON

HINTON HOUSE Classroom Activities

First published in 2009 by

Hinton House Publishers Ltd,
Newman House, 4 High Street, Buckingham, MK18 1NT, UK

T +44 (0)1280 822557 F +44 (0)560 313 5274
E info@hintonpublishers.com

www.hintonpublishers.com

Printed in the United Kingdom by Hobbs the Printers Ltd

British Library Cataloguing in Publication Data

Paterson, Kathy

3-minute motivators : more than 120 activities to help you reach, teach and achieve!
1. Creative activities and seat work 2. Motivation in education
I. Title II. Three-minute motivators
371.3

ISBN 978 1 906531 00 3

This adaptation of *3 Minute Motivators, More than 100 simple ways to reach, teach, and achieve more than you ever imagined*, by Kathy Paterson, is published by arrangement with Pembroke Publishers, Canada.

Contents

Conversation

Brainstorm

Introduction: A Touch of Magic

This is a book about magic! As every teacher or group leader knows, running a group involves an element of magic – in the persona of the leader, the presentation of the subject, or the motivation of group members. Without a touch of magic, teaching is mundane, classes are uninspired, lessons are less powerful and more forgettable. Consider the following:

> *Before …*
> The class is restless. As Miss Black, the teacher, attempts to walk them through the steps for solving the problem, she notes that several are whispering, a couple are daydreaming, another is engaged in annoying the person in front, and most have that familiar vacant 'no-one-home' stare. The brilliant spring sun shining through the window is definitely much more engaging than the teacher. She stops talking to see if they will refocus; most don't even seem to notice that she has stopped her presentation.

Teachers will recognise this scenario. It's safe to say that most, if not all, have experienced similar situations and probably are, with increasing frequency, struggling with 'UUSS' – Unmotivated/Unfocused Student Syndrome!

Why? What is making it so difficult for us to reach or teach our classes? Is there some way to wake them up, to switch them on, to keep them involved and stimulated? Is there a secret method for competing with the highly technological worlds of our students, where they are bombarded with sensual stimuli on a daily basis?

I think there is – consider this 'after' image:

> *After …*
> Miss Black shakes her tambourine loudly. All eyes immediately turn to her and talking ceases. Her pre-established and reinforced cue has done its job well. Then she says quietly, 'I can see I have lost most of you. Time to refocus! A little game … 'The group is interested. They are familiar with the concept of refocussing and enjoy these brief interjections. 'Turn to a neighbour,' Miss Black continues. 'Let's play "Shake It!"' [see page 69]. Immediately, the class is completely engaged in the activity, laughing, talking, and attempting to 'shake' the number called by the teacher. After about a minute, Miss Black interrupts the activity by once more shaking the tambourine. 'Thanks for stopping on the cue,' she says. 'Now that we've shaken out a bit of that excess energy, it's time to return to the problem I was talking to you about …

'The group, refocused, returns to the task. This time all eyes are on the teacher.

The teacher in this scenario used a little magic to refocus her group; she provided an escape for excess energy then efficiently drew the students back into her lesson. She used a 3-Minute Motivator. 3-Minute Motivators are simple activities that can be use with any age group, and with any diversity found in the classroom. I have even experienced great success in using them with university students and adults at conferences and workshops.

3-Minute Motivators is a collection of these concise activities that can be carried out *at* desks, *beside* desks, or *near* desks, with minimum or no teacher preparation, making use of few props other than the occasional paper and pencil. The actions are designed to involve the whole group in interesting, highly motivating ways, for approximately three minutes, then to refocus them on the task at hand.

But why are such activities necessary? Shouldn't students have intrinsic motivation to learn? Shouldn't they want to grow intellectually? Don't they appreciate the personal need for development as human beings? I believe the answer to each question is 'yes'; unfortunately, there are so many high-level, sense-bombarding, almost mind-numbing distractions in today's society that classroom learning can appear boring, inauthentic and monotonous.

Consider the pupils' world. How can young people be excited and motivated by what they often see as a dreary and lacklustre curriculum, when they are inundated with MP3 players, cell phones, handheld game systems and countless highly technological video games? How can they pay attention to a lesson when they are tempted daily by a wealth of stimulating information at their fingertips via the Internet? How can they sustain single-mindedness for schoolwork when they are eager to get back to their cell phone/camera/game and home entertainment system?

These days, it takes a touch of magic to keep classes inspired and focused. *3-Minute Motivators* attempts to address this issue by offering a wealth of motivating activities ready for instant use in any classroom. In addition, most of these motivators can be readily adapted to be used as anticipatory activities for a wide variety of lessons. Once you have experimented with a few of them, I think you will agree that they are, indeed, magical. Use them with an open mind; have fun!

1 Using 3-Minute Motivators with Your Group

More Than Just Motivation

What exactly *is* a 3-Minute Motivator? It is a quick activity, directed by the teacher, in which groups *want* to participate because they see it as a game, appreciating the inherent play and fun. Whether it involves competition, cooperation or individual thought or action, it provides a much-needed break from an undertaking that has lost the group's interest, and then re-concentrates attention and energy back to the teaching or learning task at hand. This re-concentration serves to point the students in the right direction once again – to refocus their attention; hence these interventions are often referred to as 'refocusers', a term that students quickly learn and accept.

Why use a 3-Minute Motivator?

- To give groups a positive break.
- To give the teacher a positive break; teachers need breaks too, and these speedy, easy-to-use activities help.
- To refocus flagging attention.
- To remove excess energy.
- To wake up lethargic minds.
- To introduce a lesson; most of the activities can have an anticipatory function.
- To reward good behaviour; they are fun, after all!

You will find many uses for the 3-Minute Motivators. Not all of the activities are unique; some of them may already be familiar to teachers. Others may be new ways to look at common activities. Use them with passion and a sense of humour as often as needed, and enjoy the positive benefits they bring to the classroom.

As with any good teaching strategy, 3-Minute Motivators all fall within a fairly consistent set of guidelines. For example, they can be satisfactorily completed within a brief amount of time. Your use of 3-Minute Motivators will be controlled by certain other basic understandings:

- There is no wrong answer.
- Variety is good and is encouraged.
- All responses are celebrated.
- Private space, both physical and emotional, is always respected.

Teachers will recognise these as important truths for all teaching, but they need to be reaffirmed with refocusers as they do with other classroom activities.

Inherent Learning

Although 3-Minute Motivators work to refocus attention, they also have inherent learning that, if the teacher chooses, can be elaborated upon. For example, the 'Shake It!' motivator (page 69) indirectly teaches and reinforces the concepts of probability and luck, while providing practice in mental addition and subtraction, and in cooperating with peers.

Look at 'Interactive Words' (page 97) as an example. Here are just a few areas (there are many more) where this activity fits conveniently into the English curriculum for Key Stage 2 (ages 8-10):

- Experimenting with rearranging of material
- Using organisational skills to clarify meaning
- Using a variety of strategies for comprehension
- Extending sight vocabulary
- Applying knowledge of graphophonic cueing systems
- Applying word analysis strategies
- Associating sounds with increasing number of vowel combinations
- Applying structural analysis cues
- Explaining relationships among letters in words
- Experimenting with words
- Using phonics knowledge
- Speaking and reading with fluency, rhythm and pace
- Working cooperatively with others.

Now consider the same motivator from the point of view of students' inherent learning. While participating in 'Interactive Words', it is quite possible that many of them would learn, quite naturally, the following:

- Words can be broken into parts
- Letters all have unique sounds
- Letter combinations have unique sounds
- Big words often contain smaller words within them
- Chanting words one letter at a time helps with spelling
- Chanting with peers is a rewarding activity

Another way to use these motivators is as quick introductory activities for specific lessons. For example, 'Shake It!' (page 69) could be used prior to a maths class on addition, subtraction or even fractions. 'Synonym Sense' (page 131) might make a motivating introduction for an English class on descriptive writing.

No doubt this same motivator could also be examined successfully from the standpoint of the other core curriculum subjects. It is always good for teachers to know that what they are doing is not only highly motivating, but that it is also viable as far as teaching the existing curriculum as well as incidental inherent learning.

Choosing a 3-Minute Motivator

Using this book is primarily a matter of choosing the best activity for any given moment and situation.

All teachers are fully aware of the importance of purpose when teaching. It is essential for a teacher – and the class – to know *why* something is being presented, revised or taught. The same goes for using 3-Minute Motivators. Quickly deciding *why* one of them is about to be used can be a determining factor in selecting the best motivator. Is it just to refocus the group, or is another purpose to be served at the same time? Certainly the single act of refocusing students so that a lesson can begin or be continued is significant, and often sufficient; however, teachers usually want to meet as many requirements as possible with every classroom action.

> *Teachers can simply select an activity at random. For example, the Maths class is 'lost' – a 3-Minute Motivator is called for! The book is opened to 'Word Tennis' (page 133) and within a couple of minutes all students are busily tossing Maths vocabulary back and forth between partners. A random choice but effective nonetheless.*

With this in mind, the question arises: 'Aren't all 3-Minute Motivators mainly designed to motivate?' Yes, but class distractions can present as restlessness, hyperactivity, fatigue or apathy (to name but a few). Moreover, many other variables come into play, such as time of day or week, the subject being interrupted by the motivator, or the teacher's attitude (i.e. current level of patience, acceptance or frustration). Therefore, the choice of the best motivator becomes a bit more difficult.

Teachers may, for example, be faced with a class who are vacant and sleepy-looking; they might choose a motivator that will 'wake them up' and provide the jolt of energy necessary to complete the assignment or lesson. Or a teacher might want to get students communicating prior to a History or Geography discussion and, perhaps because it is Friday afternoon and it's raining outside, the class is noisy and restless – in this case a motivator that involves sitting and speaking may be what is required.

> *Skim or scan the activities described in the different sections, highlight or tab the ones you find most interesting or most appropriate for your group, then keep the book readily available for instant access.*

To simplify the process of finding the right motivator for any situation, the activities have been organised into groups, and then further classified into types. For example, the 'At Your Desks' group of motivators all require the minimum of physical movement and are divided into two types: 'Calm Down' motivators involve being still and thinking (see page 15); 'Pencil & Paper' activities require the group to use these tools to complete the tasks (see page 31). For descriptions of the different types of motivators in the

'Up and At 'Em' group of more action-oriented activities see page 49 for the 'Get Moving' activities, page 71 for 'Act, Don't Speak', and page 85 for the 'Words and Movement' type. 3-Minute Motivators in the 'Let's Communicate' group are divided into types that focus on 'Single Words & Sounds' (page 95), 'Conversation' (page 111) and 'Brainstorm' (page 127). Finally, the last group of motivators can be used as extended activities that go 'Beyond the Three-Minute Mark' (page 141).

When choosing a 3-Minute Motivator from the more than 120 in this book, your best tool may be the '3-Minute Motivators at a Glance' table on pages 6–9. A quick scan of the table will give you an idea of the nature of each motivator and any particular subjects it might be most useful to address.

Many motivators have no specific subject affinity, or have a cross-curricular nature, indicated by the Subject label 'Any'.

Suggested Subjects

Many of the activities are more appropriate for one subject than another, so suggestions for appropriate curriculum subjects have been listed both in the '3-Minute Motivators at a Glance' table (pages 6–9) and on each activity. While not intended to limit use of any specific motivator to the subjects suggested, the labels indicate the subject most directly addressed. Keep in mind, however, that any motivator can be used with, or during, any subject.

You should note that all the activities involve some sort of communication, and all address most strands of the English curriculum.

Size of Group

Each of the motivators has been categorised as *Individual*, *Partners*, *Small Group* or *Whole Group*, allowing teachers to narrow their choices. If groups are being too social, for example, perhaps a motivator listed as *Individual* would be more effective than one that involves partner or small-group work.

3-Minute Motivators that are performed alone by each person, without conferring in any way with peers, are listed as 'Individual'. Some activities involve individuals contributing to, being a part of, or helping to complete a task that involves the whole class; these motivators are labelled 'Individual as part of Whole Group'. 3-Minute Motivators that require working in pairs are listed as 'Partners'. In some instances, partners work together to compete with the whole class, challenging other pairs in a competitive way; these activities are labelled 'Partners as part of Whole Group'.

When asking the group to find partners or form small groups, it is often most expedient to get 'neighbours', or those adjacent to each other to work together. You may wish to mix things up by suggesting that individuals pair with someone other than the person with whom they usually work. Heterogeneous mixing is often advantageous, and the low-risk nature of these activities lends itself to such combinations.

Keep in mind that these labels are just suggestions; most motivators can be altered to work individually or otherwise.

Props

Contributing to your choice of activity may be whether or not you need to acquire and distribute materials to use.

A few of the 3-Minute Motivators suggest the use of music. The music usually referred to is of the slow, calming genre often found on yoga music, relaxation or environmental CDs. Some classical music will also work. The key is to keep the music soft and soothing, so it operates in the background to set mood. Be sure the music has no lyrics. Please note, however, that with the exception of 'Hearing Colours' (page 18), all motivators will work well without music.

Other props may be as simple as pencil and paper, a coin or flash cards. Prop lists have been used to simplify your choice. In a hurry? Avoid an activity with a prop.

Extending the Activities

'Follow Up' and 'Showcase' ideas provided for some activities. A suggestion to 'Follow Up' means that the activity is a good one for a brief follow-up discussion. To keep within the 3-Minute part of the definition (necessary if lesson flow is to be maintained), a 60-second 'discuss with a neighbour' is suggested.

If the motivator has an 'Extended Follow Up' outlined, this indicates an activity that will work well with a longer, more in-depth discussion and perhaps lead to writing (e.g., creative or reflective writing, a story starter or sequenced directions) or representation (e.g., creating a poster or visual, a puppet presentation, drama or role play). Suggestions are listed for some of these 'Extended Follow Ups'; however, these are merely suggestions. No one knows your group better than you, and your ideas for Extended Follow Ups are limitless.

When using an Extended Follow Up at the end of the 3-Minute Motivator, you can say, 'Remember what you did (thought/visualised/ said, etc.) and we'll come back to that after we finish our lesson'. Some of the 3-Minute Motivators make use of lists of ideas, word combinations, situations, themes, etc. It is often difficult to generate instant inventories on the spur of the moment; therefore, it may be an idea to transfer some of the more commonly used lists to cards and keep them in a box for reference.

Some 3-Minute Motivators include suggestions to 'Showcase'. This indicates that this particular activity could be shared with the group. The showcase can be as simple as 30-seconds for individuals to show the rest of the group the products of their activity, to an elaborate presentation with other groups and parents, as part of an open day or concert. Often, young people enjoy showing off something they feel is cool or amusing, so why not encourage their natural desire to let others see what they have done?

The time allowed for a 'Showcase' should usually be within the three-minute proscription. We're talking about quick, snappy presentations here. Not every group member will be able to showcase every time, so you will need to be aware of turn-taking and equal opportunity. If everyone wants to showcase a particular activity, the best approach would be to point out that this will happen are when the interrupted lesson has been completed, thereby avoid losing the flow of the lesson.

3-Minute Motivators at a Glance

Motivator	Page	Suggested Subjects
At Your Desks: Calm Down		
Belly Breathing	16	PSHE
Collecting Clouds	17	Science
Hearing Colours	18	Art; PSHE
Magic Carpet	19	English; Art
Imagine This	20	Any
Time Machine	21	Science
Chocolate & Bricks	22	Any, especially PSHE
Grounding Exercise	23	Any; Use pre-test or exam
Hug-a-Tree	24	Science; PSHE
Silent Scream	25	PSHE; History & Geography
Absolutely Nothing!	26	Any
The Key	27	English
Lift Off!	28	Science
Zen Garden	29	Art; PSHE
Telescope	30	Science
At Your Desks: Pencil & Paper		
Box Me In	32	Any
Circles & Squares	33	Science; Maths
Crosses & Noughts	34	Any
Letter Scramble	35	English
4-Word Lotto	36	Any
Never-Ending Line	37	Art; Maths; Science
Draw My Words	38	Art; Science; English
Number Madness	39	Maths
Written Rumour	40	English
Shared-Pen Stories	41	English
Zoom-Out	42	Science
Scrabble Scramble	43	English; Any
Add-Ons	44	Any
Blind Draw	45	PSHE; English; History & Geography
Snow-Globe Drawings	46	Any
Mirror Images	47	English; Science; Maths

Up and At 'Em: Get Moving		
Open – Shut – Shake	50	Any: fine motor control
Puppet Master	51	English; History & Geography
The Big Yawn	52	Any
Glass Blower	53	Science; History & Geography
Levitating Arms	54	Science
Life Rhythms	55	PSHE; PE
Thunderstorm	56	Science; History & Geography
Cold – Hot – Not	57	Any
Stuck!	58	Science
False Freeze	59	Any
Heads or Tails	61	Maths
Ice Cube	62	Science; English
Number Shakes	63	Maths
Lucky Hi/Lo	64	Maths
Monkey See, Monkey Do	65	Any: sequencing skills
Musical Punching Bags	66	Any
Magic Mirrors	67	Science
Tap It To Me	68	English
Shake It!	69	Any
Up and At 'Em: Act, Don't Speak		
Fast Feet	72	PE; PSHE
Melt	73	Science
Balancing Act	74	Science; Maths; PE
Bump on the Head	75	Any
Knocking Knees	76	Music; English
Wide – Hide	77	Any
Morphing Madness	78	PE; Science; Art
Do This! Do That!	79	Any
As the Circle Turns	80	PSHE
Lean on Me	81	PSHE; PE
Lump of Clay	82	Art
Ages of Humanity	83	PSHE; English
Up and At 'Em: Words & Movement		
Move It	86	Any; PE
Walk This Way	87	Any; PE
Wrangle Tangle	88	Any; PE
Explosion!	89	Any
The Old Duke Revisited	90	Any
Meet & Greet	91	Any

Mad Milling	92	History & Geography; English
Kodak Moments	93	Any
Let's Communicate: Single Words & Sounds		
Talk-a-Lot	96	Any
Interactive Words	97	English; Any
Oscar	98	English
Count-Off	99	Maths
Hip-Hip-Hooray!	100	English
Chant-Along	101	PSHE; English
Animal Farm	102	Science
Punctuate This!	103	English
Alphabet Pyramid	104	English; Maths; Any
Popcorn	105	Science; Any
Clap 3	106	Maths
The Numbered Letter	107	English; Maths
If You're Happy …	108	Any
Quick Catch	109	Any
Let's Communicate: Conversation		
Song Speak	112	English; Music; History & Geography
I Am You	113	PSHE; History & Geography
Alphabet Game	114	English; Any
Slow-Mo	115	Any
A Quantity of Questions	116	Any
You Did What?	117	English
You DON'T Say!	118	Any
'Yes, But' Pet Peeves	119	English; PSHE
Glad Game	120	PSHE
Just a Minute	121	Any
Fortunately / Unfortunately	122	Any
I Appreciate …	123	PSHE; History & Geography
May There Be …	124	Any
Third-Person Talk	125	English
Hi-Lo Speak	126	Any
Let's Communicate: Brainstorm		
2-for-10 Tales	128	English
Point Please?	129	History & Geography; English
And the Real Meaning Is …	130	English
Synonym Sense	131	English; Any
Go-Togethers	132	Any
Word Tennis	133	English; Any
Quick Questions	134	Any

Big Word / Small Word	135	English
Excuses, Excuses	136	Any
Break-Up	137	English
If They Could Talk …	138	Any
First & Last	139	English
Beyond the Three-Minute Mark		
Obstacle Course	142	Any
Let's Quiggle	143	English; Science; Maths
Give Me a Clue	144	Science; Maths; English; PSHE
The Rule Rules!	145	History & Geography; Maths; English
Back Talk	146	History & Geography; Maths
Shake My Hand	147	PSHE; Maths; Science
Tell It Like It Is	148	History & Geography; English
Sense or Nonsense?	149	English; Any
It's MY Story!	150	English; History & Geography
The Expert	151	PSHE; Science; English
And the Action Is …	152	English; Science; History & Geography
Action Telephone	153	English; History & Geography

3-Minute Motivators in Action

Once you have chosen a 3-Minute Motivator, take a few minutes first to read it through. Note that suggested spoken instructions, words you could say to the group, are presented in *italics*. The instructions are presented in this manner to facilitate use (all you need to do is read the brief notes to the class) and keep the motivators simple and quick to use. Naturally, the instructions provided do not need to be used word-for-word; these are guidelines only. A quick read of the entire motivator will probably be sufficient for instant use.

Any non-italicised text within the activity steps (presented as a bullet list) supplies additional directions. It may, for example, suggest that you 'signal to start,' or 'remind the group when they have 30 seconds remaining'. Unlike the italicised instructions, these are not meant to be read to the class.

Use the full list of steps on page 12 as a handy reference to using a 3-Minute Motivator. It includes the entire process, from Attention Signal to Concluding and Refocusing.

When introducing a 3-Minute Motivators to your class, it is good to reinforce these ideas:

- *There is no wrong answer.*
- *Variety is good and is encouraged.*
- *All responses are celebrated.*
- *Private space, both physical and emotional, will always be respected.*

The Attention Signal

As every teacher knows, if the group isn't paying attention, teaching is a waste of time. So it is with 3-Minute Motivators. The group must be paying attention when the teacher introduces the activity. Therefore, the activity should be preceded by an attention signal that has been already established in the class. Some excellent signals include:

- A short blast of a whistle
- Use of any percussion instrument
- Use of specific piece of music
- A clapping sequence led by you
- Raising your hand and waiting silently until the whole group has raised their hands
- Rapping a squeaky hammer (or anything resembling a gavel) on your desk (This is my personal favourite as it simulates a courtroom, with the teacher as judge. My huge squeaky hammer works well with groups at *any* level – even adults!)

As with any situation in which a specific reaction is expected to a specific signal, the use of the signal must be first introduced, then cultivated and reinforced:

1. Introduce the signal and explain its purpose.
   When you hear this sound, you should immediately stop what you are doing and look at me.
2. Practice
   Everybody talk to a neighbour and be prepared to freeze when you hear the sound.
3. Reinforce
   - *Excellent! You all stopped talking and looked at me. That's exactly what I wanted you to do. This helps me because …*
   - *I'm so glad you all remembered to freeze at the signal and look at me. Now I know you are ready to …*
   - *Thank you for freezing when you heard the sound. That's great! I know you want to …*

Repeat steps 2 and 3 frequently for a few days, reinforcing consistently. Eventually, obeying the attention signal should become a classroom habit and can be reinforced intermittently.

The Importance of Concluding and Refocusing

Perhaps the most important aspect of successfully using a 3-Minute Motivator is the manner in which it is ended. A smooth transition is necessary to enable you to bring the group back from an activity to the previously interrupted task or lesson. Although it takes only a few moments to make this crucial shift in focus, without it the group may be left wondering what they have just done, why they did it and where they are supposed to be going as a result.

Once the motivator is finished to your satisfaction:

1 Signal for attention.

2 Quickly state why the refocuser/motivator was carried out. *I had the feeling none of you were really listening to the information about … so we …* (summarise the activity).

3 Concisely state current expectations for return to work. *Now that you've had a chance to burn some energy (talk to a neighbour/move around a bit …), I need you to return to lesson and give it your full attention.*

4 Provide positive reinforcement for return-to-work behaviours.

5 Continue with the lesson or remind students what they were supposed to be doing before the motivator. *We were learning about … and I was explaining how to …*

This entire 'speech' should take no more than 30 seconds. Students will quickly learn that, although they have fun with the motivators, they are expected to return to work immediately following them.

Class Participation

If some group members are reluctant to cooperate and participate, even when the activity is presented as a game, allow them to choose to sit quietly at their desks and simply observe. It has been my experience that, after observing just once or twice, most individuals want to take part in activities, especially those that allow them imaginative freedom. On the other hand, many of the 3-Minute Motivators are entertaining to watch, so less outgoing students may choose to enjoy them from this point of view; they still benefit from the refocusing quality of the motivator.

> *Concluding a 3-Minute Motivator follows a what – why – what pattern: what was done, why it was done, what is to be done now.*

The main difficulty may be with those who wish to disrupt the class during the more quiet activities. The very nature of the 'Calm Down' 3-Minute Motivators will be jeopardised if even a single student is noisy. Teachers must deal with these situations in whatever way works best for them, keeping in mind that the success of calming activities depends on a room that is quiet for up to three minutes. If the student cannot or will not meet the three-minute criterion, it may be best to remove him or her for the short duration of the activity.

Some motivators lend themselves to unusual competitive challenges; these can be enhanced with the addition of small prizes. It is not the size or quality of the prize that counts, but rather the idea of the prize that is, in itself, motivating. What's magical about the prizes associated with 3-Minute Motivators is that often they are won by those who seldom excel in other classroom pursuits.

Steps for Using a 3-Minute Motivator

1. Give the signal to gain attention.
2. Briefly explain why the motivator is being used.

   I have lost you …

   You seem restless …

   I can see you need a break …

   You seem to need some talk time …
3. Explain the activity, using the directions included in each 3-Minute Motivator.
4. Remind the group not to begin until you signal them to do so, and to stop or freeze again on signal.
5. Signal to begin.
6. Present the 3-Minute Motivator, using the script provided.
7. Signal to stop.
8. Conclude and refocus by quickly summarising what was done and why.

   We were all a bit restless so we just played … Now that you've used up a bit of energy, it's time to return to …

   You seemed sleepy and many of you were not paying attention, so we played … Now that you're all awake, let's get back to …

   I felt the need for a quick break, so we played … Now we can get back to …

Tips for Teaching with 3-Minute Motivators

- Make it fun, not punishment! Better to say, 'Time for a refocuser. This is a little game ... ' than to say, 'No one is paying attention and you are all talking, so we have to do something to change that ... ' The word 'game' is the catch for kids.
- Always begin with your pre-established attention signal and end with a return to the interrupted or ensuing lesson.
- Always tell the group *why* you chose to use a 3-Minute Motivator.
- Stick to the three-minute time frame as much as possible (unless you have a reason for varying the process). If you wish to follow up a motivator, keep it to about one minute, or say, 'Remember what you just did/thought/saw /heard ... and we'll talk about it after we finish our ... [whatever you interrupted for the refocuser]'.
- Use the term 'refocuser' when referring to 3-Minute Motivators. The jargony term appeals to kids, and they start to look forward to the chance to 'refocus'.
- Remember the element of surprise. Keep your motivators fresh. Avoid using the same one again and again, and choose activities from different sections regularly. Mix them up.
- Note that directions for the teacher to say/read presented in *italics* mean that a motivator can be used instantaneously if necessary.
- It's a good idea to familiarise yourself with a few activities from each section, but don't feel you need to memorise the teacher's speaking directions.

/ cont ...

Tips *continued*

- Don't feel forced to read class instructions exactly as they are written. These are simply suggestions. You can easily add your own flavour and make the motivators your own.
- Be sure the directions you provide (following the attention signal) are specific and exact. Remember that you want to reduce chaos, not create it.
- Use 3-Minute Motivators proactively rather than reactively. It is better to stop the lesson and interject a motivator when attention is just starting to wane, than when behaviour has escalated to the classroom bedlam all teachers face from time to time.
- Remember that the 'Follow Up', 'Extended Follow Up' and 'Showcase' ideas are suggestions only; you can choose to use them or ignore them.
- Remember that although a motivator may involve props, it will work well without them.
- Don't worry if a motivator flops! Just admit defeat and return to the lesson. (Even an activity that flops serves, in its own way, to refocus.)
- Keep a record (perhaps using the '3-Minute Motivators at a Glance' table) of motivators that you have used effectively or ineffectively, those you would like to use again or would prefer to forget. Since the book contains so many motivators, this easy record-keeping will simplify future use of the activities.

2 At Your Desks

Calm Down

The motivators in this section require the least amount of physical activity as the group remain seated silently throughout. With the teacher leading, students engage their imaginations in interesting, often unusual, ways. That these refocusing activities involve a degree of meditation, of quiet reflection and rumination, will quickly become obvious to teachers. What may be less obvious is how successfully students of all ages can handle, learn from and appreciate such deliberations.

These motivators are most effective for situations where the group have been very active; the teacher's goal is to calm them down in preparation for a more concentrated pursuit. For example, students may be off-task, talkative, out-of desk, unfocused, or actively disinterested in the lesson or job at hand. There may be a general state of disorganisation or hyperactivity in the room, or there may simply be too much contagious energy to allow for effective teaching and subsequent learning to take place.

- To capitalise on the goal of relaxation the teacher should use a quiet, soothing, often monotone voice when providing the direction or presenting the scenarios. This is not a time for high passion and enthusiasm, but for firm, tranquil and composed intervention.
- Some of these calming motivators ('Belly Breathing', 'Hug-a-Tree', 'Grounding Exercise', 'Zen Garden') work well before important or intense seated activity, such as tests or exams. They may serve to reduce anxiety and encourage maximum effort.
- Most of the refocusers in this section take the form of 'guided imagery', as the teacher calmly guides the thinking and internal visualisation of the students. If some students reject this type of imagery, at least they will be sitting quietly with their eyes closed for the duration, and that in itself can serve as a positive experience.
- Most of these motivators work best on an individual basis; however, you may wish to follow up by encouraging quiet discussion.
- The opportunities for relevant discussion or follow-up writing are many, even if the particular refocuser does not include Follow Up or Showcase notes. Neither of these literacy activities will lessen the effectiveness of the relaxing refocuser.

*These motivators may be useful on days when, for example, weather prohibits going outside for break-time and groups suffer from cabin fever, or when weekends or holidays are near and attention is elsewhere.
Or students may just have returned from a lively physical education class, an assembly, or other dynamic gathering that has invigorated them.*

1 Belly Breathing

Any

Art

English

History & Geography

Maths

PE

PSHE

Science

Objective To breathe deeply and with control.

Note 'Belly Breathing' can be used *before* other motivators in this section, as an additional calming activity.

- *Sit quietly at your desk, hands folded.*
- *Close your eyes.*
- *Breathe normally.*
- *Now focus on your breathing: slowly* **in** *to a count of 5, hold for 5, slowly* **out** *for a count of 5.*
- *When you inhale, visualise yourself getting bigger and lighter. Air is rushing in to fill all your body cavities: chest, stomach, back, shoulders ...*
- *When you hold your breath, visualise yourself getting lighter and lighter, even levitating.*
- *When you exhale, visualise yourself squeezing your lungs, getting rid of every bit of air, pushing it all out through your mouth. (This might make you cough, and that's okay. It just means you are getting all the dead air out.)*
- Remind students to keep their eyes closed, to continue breathing like this for about two minutes, and to silently count the seconds to themselves. Talk about 'filling up like a balloon' when inhaling, and 'squeezing your diaphragm down to your hips and sucking your tummy in' when exhaling.
- Allow the group to continue for as long as they remain focused, or up to a maximum of two minutes, then say, *This will be your last breath. Slowly fill yourself up, count. Exhale and, as you curl down into yourself like a balloon losing all its air, you feel quiet, calm, relaxed ...*

Individuals

Partners

Small Group

Whole Group

2 Collecting Clouds

Objective	To attain a sense of calm by visualising clouds.
Props	Calming music from yoga, environmental sounds, relaxation CDs

- *Sit comfortably, feet on floor, heads on desks, arms comfortably wherever you want them.*
- *Close your eyes and focus on your breathing.* Allow about 15 seconds for this.
- *Now, think of clouds – a beautiful clear blue sky and lots of clouds.*
- *What do your clouds look like? See them in your mind. Really look at them.*
- *What shapes are they? Are they changing shape?*
- *Are they moving?*
- *Imagine you are floating on one of the clouds.*
- *What does it feel like?*
- *What can you see?*
- Allow this to continue silently for up to 30 seconds or until you note restlessness, then continue: *Now come back down to earth, but keep feeling the gentle movement of the clouds as you sit up quietly.*

Any | Art | English | History & Geography | Maths | PE | PSHE | **Science**

Individuals | Partners | Small Group | Whole Group

Extended Follow Up	Written work or illustration of the activity.
Showcase	Presentation and group discussion of results of extended follow-up.

3 Hearing Colours

Any
Art
English
History & Geography
Maths
PE
PSHE
Science

Objective To attach imaginary colours to sounds.

Props Calming music from yoga, environmental sounds, relaxation CDs, even classical music

- *Sit quietly at your desk, feet on the floor, heads on desktops. Close your eyes.*
- *You are going to hear some music. Listen to it and see in your mind the colours you think of when you hear the music.*
- Play the music. Wait for 10 seconds then say, *What colours do you see?*
- *Think colour. Does the music make you think of green? Or maybe pink?*
- *Concentrate on the colours of the rainbow and try to visualise which shades this music makes you think of.*
- *Breathe deeply and think colour.*
- *I am going to stop the music. When I do, you will sit up quietly and think of the colour or colours you saw in your mind.*

Individuals
Partners
Small Group
Whole Group

Follow Up The group can quietly discuss visualised colours; or you can conduct a quick survey of the predominant colours.

4 Magic Carpet

Any
Art
English
History & Geography
Maths
PE
PSHE
Science

Objective To experience sensory awareness.

- *Sit quietly, feet on floor, head on hands on desk. Close your eyes and breathe deeply.*
- *I am going to take you away from here on a magic-carpet ride.*
- *Imagine you are not sitting at your desk; you are on a beautiful carpet. Try to imagine the following:*
- *What does your carpet look like? What colour is it? What does it feel like?*
- *Now the carpet is going to start moving. It is slowly rising up, slowly … rising … getting higher.*
- *What does it feel like now? Can you feel the gentle movement?*
- *Pay attention to the gentle breeze in your face as your special carpet moves higher and higher.*
- *You feel very comfortable. You are high above the clouds. You are totally relaxed as your carpet sails along like a bird in the air.*
- *Now imagine where you are going. This is your carpet so you can make it go wherever you want it to. Where would you like your carpet to take you?*
- *You can look down if you want to, in your mind. What do you see? Where are you going?*
- *Now I'm going to stop talking and I want you to remain on your carpets for 60 seconds, just flying wherever you want to, feeling happy and peaceful.*
- After 60 seconds bring them back by saying, *Now you are going to come back to earth. Let your carpet come down gently, slowly, until you are back in your seat.*

Individuals
Partners
Small Group
Whole Group

Follow Up *Discuss details of your trip with someone else.*

Extended Follow Up Class discussion leading to a literacy assignment.

Showcase Class display and discussion of artwork, stories and descriptions.

5 Imagine This

Any

Art

English

History & Geography

Maths

PE

PSHE

Science

Objective To experience the sights, smells, and sounds of an imaginary outing.

- *Sit quietly at your desk, feet on floor, heads on desks. Close your eyes and breathe deeply.*
- *I am going to take you to an imaginary place. I want you to concentrate on everything you see, hear, smell and feel. First just concentrate on your breathing – in – out – in – out . . .*
- *You are lost in the wilderness.* (See box for additional Situations.) *It is a lovely day, but you are lost.*
- *Look around in your mind. What do you see? What do you hear? What time of day is it? How do you feel?*
- *Walk around slowly. Look at everything. Pay attention to the sounds. Pay attention to the smells.*
- Continue in this manner, focusing on different aspects of sensory awareness depending on the 'location' or theme chosen. The idea is to force students to 'be' in this setting and really focus on it in their minds.
- As this motivator is intended to be soothing, keep the images positive. Avoid taking the students' thoughts to negative situations.

Individuals

Partners

Small Group

Whole Group

Follow Up A follow up is strongly encouraged for this activity. This can be quick (assuming you want to return to your previous lesson). Simply ask the group to describe where they were and what any dominant images were.

Extended Follow Up Since students can experience very strong images, they like to describe these either with the group or on paper. The images might make ideas for future writing: at this point they can be quickly jotted down in note books; a whole-class discussion could take place prior to a literacy task.

Suggested Situations
• In Space • In the Arctic • At a farm • Under the sea
• At an amusement park • In a magic kingdom • On top of a ski slope
• On the moon • In a plane above the mountains • Inside a huge tree
• At the beach • In a meadow filled with flowers

6 Time Machine

Objective To imagine travelling forwards or backwards in time.

- *Sit quietly at your desks, feet on the floor, heads resting comfortably on your desks.*
- *Breathe deeply; focus on your breathing. Relax completely.*
- *You are very lucky today. You are going to go inside a time machine. Just keep listening carefully to find out how to do this.*
- *First imagine where you'd like to go. Into the past? To the age of dinosaurs or cave men? Or into the future? On a rocket ship? On an alien planet?*
- *Take a few breaths to decide silently where you will travel.*
- Wait for about 15 seconds. Then say, *I will count back from ten and, when I get to one, your time machine will whisk you off to your chosen time and place. Get ready – 10, 9, 8, 7, 6, 5, 4, 3, 2, 1. Go!*
- Wait for a few seconds then say, *You are there.*
- *Breathe deeply and take time to look around. What do you see? What do you hear? Smell? Feel?*
- *For the next 60 seconds really pay attention to this magical time and place. Nothing bad can happen here because you chose a perfect place. Just enjoy it.*
- Wait for about 60 seconds, then say, *When I count to ten, your time machine will start to bring you home again. Here we go – 1, 2, 3, 4, 5, 6, 7, 8, 9, 10!*
- *Keep your eyes closed for a few seconds and remember everything you saw and felt.*
- *Now slowly sit up and open your eyes.*

Follow Up A follow up discussion is strongly advised with this activity. This can be quick (assuming you want to return to your previous lesson). Simply ask students to discuss where they were and what any dominant images were.

Extended Follow Up Since students can experience very strong images, they like to share these either with peers or on paper. The images might make ideas for future writing, drama activities, or art projects: ideas could be quickly jotted down in note books; a whole-class discussion could take place prior to a descriptive task.

7 Chocolate & Bricks

Any

Art

English

History & Geography

Maths

PE

PSHE

Science

Objective To release frustrations and appreciate something good.

- *Sit comfortably, feet on the floor, hands together, eyes closed. Relax and breathe deeply.*
- *I want you to start to think of something or someone that really annoys you or makes you angry. Now concentrate on the bad feeling – the anger and frustration. Feel it: you are all tense and angry. Feel it in your stomach, in your head – everywhere. I am going to give you 10 seconds to really experience that bad feeling.*
- Wait 10 seconds. *Now take that nasty feeling and cement it inside a solid brick.*
- *Push it into a brick. Close the opening with cement. Now you have a heavy, hard brick with the bad feeling inside*
- *Now comes the fun part. In your mind you get to blow up that brick – wait until I give you the Blast signal. When I say 'Blast!', you will imagine blowing the brick into millions of tiny pieces. The bad feeling will be completely gone.*
- *Get ready – look closely at the brick with your annoying thing inside it. BLAST!*
- *Keep your eyes closed.*
- *Now think of something or someone that makes you very happy. See that thing or person; feel the good feeling; really try to experience the good feeling you get from the thing or person. You feel warm and comfy inside. You are smiling to yourself. I'll give you a few seconds to really feel the good feeling.*
- Wait for about 10 seconds. *Now take the feeling that the good thing gives you and cover it in chocolate. Look at the good feeling all covered in chocolate.*
- *What sort of a shape does it make? Can you smell that delicious chocolate?*
- *Now, when I tell you to, in your mind you are going to eat the chocolate. When you do that, the good feeling will stay inside you, making you all warm and tingly.*
- *Ready? Look at the chocolate-covered good feeling. Eat it.*

Individuals

Partners

Small Group

Whole Group

Extended Follow Up This is an excellent activity to follow with individual written reflections. Guiding questions might be:

- How did it feel when you blew up the brick?
- How did it feel when you ate the chocolate?
- Were the feelings different? The same?

8 Grounding Exercise

Objective To experience a total sense of calm by using a grounding or centring- of-self technique borrowed from Eastern philosophies.

Notes This is perfect for pre-exam situations. Attempt to speak in a slow, quiet monotone for this exercise.

- *Sit comfortably, feet flat on floor. Don't slouch; sit up straight. Put your hands together on your desk.*
- *Move slightly away from the back of your seat so that you are not leaning against it.*
- *Relax your tongue. Let it lie gently in your mouth. Relax your jaw.*
- *Close your eyes and breathe deeply and quietly – in through your nose, out through your mouth. In – out. In – out …*
- Wait for 10 seconds before continuing. *Now imagine you see a beautiful golden ball floating before you. Look at it – it's swirling and shining and sparkling. So beautiful.*
- *Watch it. Really look at in your mind. Keep thinking, 'Beautiful golden ball … '*
- Repeat these phrases as many times as needed to allow students to calm down. You will need to use your judgment here, remembering that not everyone will have the same experience.
- *Now look closely. The beautiful golden ball is moving toward you – closer, closer.*
- *It is moving* **inside** *you, right into your stomach.*
- *The beautiful golden ball is* **in** *your stomach* (or *tummy*). *It is making you feel warm, relaxed, wonderful …*
- *Feel the ball filling you with golden light, making you calm, confident, relaxed and happy …*
- *Keep enjoying the feel of the golden ball in your stomach until you hear the Stop signal.*
- Wait for up to 60 seconds then say, *Stop. Let the ball go and open your eyes.*

Follow Up A quick discussion of 'how it felt' is useful here, especially if this is the first time this technique has been used.

Extended Follow Up Excellent to extend to written reflection. For many students, this technique may be quite surprising and refreshing.

Any
Art
English
History & Geography
Maths
PE
PSHE
Science

Individuals
Partners
Small Group
Whole Group

9 Hug-a-Tree

Any

Art

English

History & Geography

Maths

PE

PSHE

Science

Objective To experience the sensory imagery of hugging a tree.

- *Sit comfortably at your desk, feet on floor.*
- *Close your eyes and stretch across your desk.*
- *Spread your arms wide, resting them on the desk.*
- *Slowly bring your arms together as if hugging a tree.*
- *Stop moving your arms when you get to the size of your tree trunk.*
- *Keep hugging the tree and in your mind, visualise what your special tree looks like, feels like, smells like.*
- *Keep hugging gently and feel the calm strength of the tree entering you, relaxing you, making you feel relaxed and peaceful.*

Individuals

Partners

Small Group

Whole Group

10 Silent Scream

Objective To demonstrate strong emotions using only body language.

- *We all have many strong feelings – emotions. Sometimes we are not able to show these because of where we are or who we are with. We are going to practice some silent emotions.*
- *Sit tall, facing the front, eyes on me. These expressions of emotions are for you only; you don't need to look at anyone else.*
- *Begin by thinking of being very sad. Think of unhappiness and feel it with your body – your eyes, your head, your chest, your hands. Breathe slowly. Very, very sad – feel it and let your body show it for 10 seconds.*
- Take the group through each of these emotions: anger, fear, worry, pride, excitement.
- Be sure to end with a positive emotion such as happiness, peacefulness, joy, relaxation or contentment.

Any | Art | English | **History & Geography** | Maths | PE | **PSHE** | Science

Individuals | Partners | Small Group | Whole Group

Follow Up A quick discussion of how it felt to show emotion without words.

Extended Follow Up Writing about an emotion that is difficult or easy to express silently.

Showcase Choose group members to read out their work based on what you know about individual students.

11 Absolutely Nothing!

Any

Art

English

History & Geography

Maths

PE

PSHE

Science

Objective To do absolutely nothing for as long as possible.

- *This is a difficult game. You are going to do* ***nothing****!*
- *Start by sitting comfortably in your chair. You can put your heads on your desks if you want to. Just be sure you are very comfortable.*
- *When I give the Start signal, you are going to freeze – not move at all, not make a single sound – for a full minute. Sounds easy doesn't it? It's not.*
- *So check to see if you are comfy and in a position you can hold without moving – not even to scratch!*
- Work up to sitting still for 60 seconds (and more). It can be difficult, especially for younger groups, to remain motionless and silent for this amount of time.

Individuals

Partners

Small Group

Whole Group

Follow Up Discuss what was difficult or easy about the game.

Extended Follow Up Challenge students to think of situations where total immobility and silence might be necessary.

12 The Key

Any

Art

English

History & Geography

Maths

PE

PSHE

Science

Objective To creatively imagine what could be done with a mysterious key.

- *Sit comfortably. You can put your heads on your desks if you want to.*
- *Close your eyes and breathe deeply. Listen to my voice.*
- *I want you to visualise – see in your mind – a huge, shiny key. The key is as large as your fist. Look at it.*
- *What shape is it?*
- *What colour?*
- *Think only about that amazing key. It will open whatever door you want.*
- *Start thinking of everything you will see when the key opens doors.*
- Wait for about 20 seconds before continuing. *Now choose just one of those doors to open. Use your magic key to open it and take yourself on a magical journey.*
- Wait about 20 seconds. *Take time to see, hear, smell, and maybe even taste everything behind your magical door. Pay attention to colour, texture, smell. Stay in your magical place until I give you the Stop signal.*

Individuals

Partners

Small Group

Whole Group

Extended Follow Up This is an excellent activity to use before creative writing, as long as some discussion occurs between the guided imagery and the writing process.

13 Lift Off!

Any
Art
English
History & Geography
Maths
PE
PSHE
Science

Objective To imagine the body levitating or lifting out of the desk into the air.

- *Sit comfortably at your desk, feet flat on the floor. Rest your head on your arms and close your eyes.*
- *Breathe deeply in through your nose, out through your mouth. Be silent and listen to my voice.*
- *You feel very heavy, like a solid rock. Heavy, heavy … Think of pressure pushing down on you – pushing hard, making you heavier and heavier.*
- *Keep thinking of the pressure and the heaviness of your body – your legs, your arms, your head …*
- Wait for about 20 seconds before continuing: *Now something magical is happening. Suddenly you feel the pressure being lifted off.*
- *Your feet and legs start to feel light. They almost lift right off the floor.*
- *Your body feels lighter and lighter.*
- *The light feeling moves into your shoulders, head, arms … Lighter, lighter …*
- *You are so light you start to feel yourself lift right off the chair in your mind – not in reality, remember. Lighter, lighter …*
- *Now imagine you are actually lifting up, rising up into the air – slowly, like a weightless bubble. Lifting, rising … Rising up, up, up … Lighter and lighter …*
- Continue coaching the group in this way for as long as you feel is appropriate, then say, *You will gently float around until you hear the Stop signal.*

Individuals
Partners
Small Group
Whole Group

Follow Up What did it feel like? Encourage a brief discussion between partners for a few seconds before returning to the interrupted activity.

14 Zen Garden

Objective To trace curved lines with fingers for up to 60 seconds.

Props Pencils and unlined paper

- *Take out a clean piece of paper, without lines, and a pencil or pen.*
- *When I give the Start signal, you will fill the paper with gently waving lines, going from the top of the page to the bottom.*
- *You will begin by drawing a single line like this.* Demonstrate by drawing a curvy line on the board. Avoid making it complicated; it should be a gentle curve such as might be seen in a Zen garden.
- *Now you will fill the page by drawing other lines close to, but not touching, the first line.*
- *Leave a space of 2cm to 3cm between the lines.*
- *Every line will follow the first line until your page is filled.*
- *When you have finished, put your pen down and sit quietly waiting for the next instruction.*
- Allow about 30 seconds for this, or until everyone has finished. Give additional guidance as necessary.
- *Now, when I give the Start signal, use your fingers to slowly follow the curved lines from the top to the bottom, over and over again.*
- *Follow the lines and focus on the gentle curves.*
- *Touch softly, gently; your fingers barely touch the paper.*
- *Keep doing this until I give the Stop signal.*

Any | **Art** | English | History & Geography | Maths | PE | **PSHE** | Science

Individuals | Partners | Small Group | Whole Group

Follow Up Quickly discuss how it felt to carry out this task. Most groups find it extremely calming.

15 Telescope

Any

Art

English

History & Geography

Maths

PE

PSHE

Science

Objective To imagine looking at an object through a very powerful telescope.

- *Sit comfortably with your feet on the floor and your heads on your arms.*
- *Close your eyes.*
- *If you prefer to sit up straight and close your eyes, that's okay too.*
- *You are very comfortable. Breathe deeply in through your nose, out through your mouth.*
- *Now I want you imagine you have in front of you a very powerful telescope. This telescope will allow you to see in great detail anything you want to see.*
- *For example you might want to look at your own hand and see all the tiny lines, colours, wrinkles … whatever.*
- *Or you might want to look at something far away, like the moon. You could see all the details of the surface of the moon.*
- *I want you to think for a few seconds about what you will examine through your telescope. Don't look through it yet. Just think of what you will examine. I'll tell you when to look through the telescope.*
- Wait for about 20 seconds, then tell the group to begin looking. Give guidance for a few seconds, then remain quiet for up to two minutes.

Individuals

Partners

Small Group

Whole Group

Follow Up Ask the group to talk about what they were examining. This should be a very quick 'once around the room' discussion.

Extended Follow Up Write about or discuss at greater length the detailed images.

Pencil & Paper

The motivators in this section continue to keep groups in their seats, but differ from 'Calm Down' activities in that they involve more active, often more stimulating, participation. As students will be required to think and react quickly using paper and pencils, these tasks tend to be more cognitive and arousing. Many of them are competitive in nature, encouraging fast reactions ('Scrabble Scramble', page 43), careful predictions ('Never-Ending Line', page 37), or directed thinking (Written Rumour, page 40). Groups love these motivators largely because creativity is encouraged in a context where no response is incorrect. They work well before lessons requiring careful drawing ('Zoom-Out', page 42), fine motor control ('Mirror Images', page 47), active listening, such as to a teacher presentation ('Draw My Words', page 38) or literacy concepts ('Letter Scramble', page 35).

Unlike the 'Calm Down' activities for individuals, these motivators all involve working with partners or in small groups:

- Often the quickest way to form pairs is to simply ask people to partner with the person behind or beside them.
- Another quick way is to have the group number-off: 1 and 3 are partners, as are 2 and 4, and so on.
- It is always a good idea to change the system regularly to encourage new relationships and provide the opportunity for all students to work with, and learn from, each other.

Useful at any time your class simply need a break, 'Pencil & Paper' activities are especially useful following a more physical class, such as a movement, PE, or Art class. In these instances, they serve as a transition from a big activity full of movement to a smaller or more focused desk-bound activity. Teachers will all have their own favourite ways to pair students, but a little advance thought as to which method will be used will prevent possible arguments and classroom disruption.

16 Box Me In

Any

Art

English

History & Geography

Maths

PE

PSHE

Science

Objective	To avoid being boxed in during a simple game of chance and cognition.

Note	This is a silent activity.

- *Sit as close together as possible. You may have to move a chair and use one desk between you for this game.*
- *You each need a pen or pencil (different colours are best); you need one piece of paper between you.*
- *Draw four dots across the page about 3cm apart, then put three dots going down the page under each of these dots, filling in a square. You will have 16 dots altogether.* Draw on the board to demonstrate a 4-by-4 square made up of dots.
- *Here's the game. Decide who will start.* Wait until everyone decides.
- *The Starter joins any two dots to make a straight line – but not diagonally. Then the other person connects any two dots, and so on.*
- *Here's the trick. The boxes represent little jails. You need to stay out of them. That means you do **not** want to be forced to draw the last line that completes a box. If you do, you must put your initial **in** that box – go to jail – and take another turn.*
- *The person with the fewest number of initials in boxes is the winner, because he or she has been to jail the least number of times.*
- *Remember that this is a silent activity.*

Individuals

Partners

Small Group

Whole Group

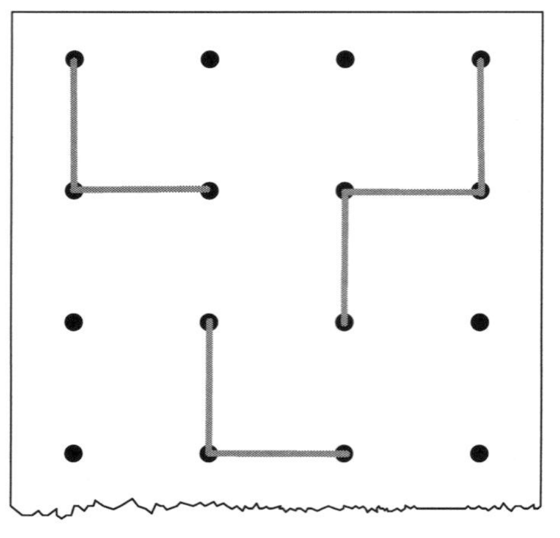

17 Circles & Squares

Objective To create, with a partner, an interesting illustration or abstract picture using only circles and squares, without speaking.

Note No speaking is allowed.

- *Decide between you who will be the circle and who will be the square.*
- *You and your partner will have two minutes to create an interesting picture.*
- *But here's the catch – you can use only your designated shape. The squares can draw only squares and the circles can draw only circles.*
- *AND … you can't talk to each other. You just have to start drawing – taking turns – and see what happens.*
- Signal to start.
- Warn the group when there are only 30 seconds left.
- Signal to stop.
- *You now have 30 seconds to discuss with your partner what your drawing could be. Maybe it's an abstract. Maybe it looks like something. Decide now.* Stop after 30 seconds.

Any

Art

English

History & Geography

Maths

PE

PSHE

Science

Individuals

Partners

Small Group

Whole Group

Follow Up Quickly allow each pair to show and name their drawing.

18 Crosses & Noughts

Any

Art

English

History & Geography

Maths

PE

PSHE

Science

Objective To play a paper and pencil game, the opposite to the familiar 'Noughts and Crosses'.

- *This game is like the game you know as* 'Noughts and Crosses' *but it's just the opposite.*
- *Start by drawing two vertical lines and two horizontal lines through them.* Demonstrate the grid on the board.
- *You now have nine empty boxes.*
- *Decide who is Cross and who is Nought.*
- *Take turns putting your signs in boxes. Your job is to avoid making a straight line with your sign.*
- *If your partner forces you to make a straight line, you're out.*

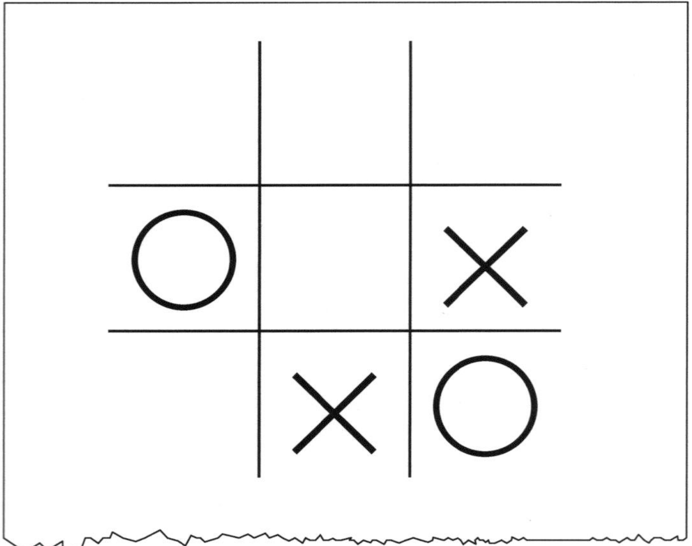

Individuals

Partners

Small Group

Whole Group

19 Letter Scramble

Objective To randomly write five letters, then add these to a partner's five letters to make words.

- *Start by each writing five letters on your page, but don't let your partner see what you're writing.*
- *Now, put together the letters you have both written, and make as many words from these letters as possible.*
- *If you both have chosen the same letter, that means you can use that letter twice in a word. Otherwise each letter can only be used once in a word.*
- *You will have two minutes. Go!*
- At the end of two minutes, count the words and find the winning pairs. Do a quick check for accuracy. Point out that a lot is dependent upon which letters they initially chose. Once the group have played this game a few times, they become expert at selecting the letters that naturally transform into the maximum number of words.

20 4-Word Lotto

- **Any (as source of words)**
- Art
- English
- History & Geography
- Maths
- PE
- PSHE
- Science

Objective To randomly select words with a partner, and take a chance that they will be the words chosen from a list by the teacher.

Props A list of 10 to 15 (or 20 to 25) words.

Notes A grid of two vertical and two horizontal lines means group can choose nine words, increasing the difficulty level. In this case, you should have 20 – 25 words from which to select.

Words can be core-subject related, word-wall related, spelling related or just randomly chosen. Teachers can have them already written on slips of paper, or the group can choose them.

Selecting lotto words from subject areas helps with vocabulary reinforcement and spelling. Choosing to provide the definitions of the words, rather than the words themselves, can help to reinforce meaning.

- *Make a large cross or grid on your page, made of two lines intersecting, forming 4 squares.*
- *From our list of words, choose any four and write one in each square.*
- *I will randomly choose a word from the list. If you have that word, draw a line through it.*
- *The first pair to have lines through all their words wins.*

- Individuals
- **Partners**
- Small Group
- Whole Group

add	~~subtract~~
equals	fraction

21 Never-Ending Line

Objective To draw a picture with a partner, sharing a single pencil and using an uninterrupted line.

Note No speaking is allowed.

- *Each pair of you should have one sheet of unlined paper and one pencil.*
- *You and your partner have to create an interesting picture – but there's a catch. Once you put the pencil on the paper, you cannot lift it again until I give the Stop signal.*
- *Your picture will be made from one continuous, never-ending line, and you'll take it in turns to make it.*
- *Every time you hear my signal, exchange the pencil. The person receiving the pencil must pick up where their partner stopped and keeps going.*
- *But there's another catch. You can't discuss what you are drawing. It just has to grow out of the line you are making.* Demonstrate or give an example using students' names.
- Signal to start. Signal every five seconds or so, for up to about two minutes.
- *Now you and your partner have 20 seconds to decide what your picture is. Then you can quickly tell the group.*

Any | **Art** | English | History & Geography | **Maths** | PE | PSHE | **Science**

Individuals | **Partners** | Small Group | Whole Group

Follow Up Invite each pair to hold up their drawing and tell everyone what it is.

22 Draw My Words

Any

Art

English

History & Geography

Maths

PE

PSHE

Science

Objective To 'copy' an illustration by listening to a partner's directions.

Note For younger groups, provide an illustration to be described. Older groups can work from nouns or verbs which can be themed.

- *Decide who will be the Speaker and who will be the Artist.*
- *All Artists must now turn away from the front of the room.* (Assuming use of a whiteboard or overhead projector, you don't want them to see the illustration or word.)
- Make the illustration or word clearly visible to the Speakers.
- *Now, Speakers, your job is to get your partner to reproduce/draw this illustration/word by giving them instructions.*
- ***But** you can't tell them what they are drawing. The only directions you can give are words for shape, lines or placement on the page.*
- *For example, you might say, 'At the top of the page draw a circle'.*
- *You have two minutes to talk your partner through the entire drawing.*
- Signal to start and stop.

Individuals

Partners

Small Group

Whole Group

Showcase Each pair shows the group their drawing. Discuss ways of giving instructions.

Possible illustrations
- Fish, mermaid, octopus, whale, jellyfish, starfish
- Rabbit, cat, dog, elephant, giraffe, turtle
- Car, truck, train, boat
- Stick people 'in action'
- Flower, tree, bird, butterfly, ladybird
- House, barn, church, tepee, tent, hut

23 Number Madness

Objective To use previously chosen numbers to arrive at teacher-provided numerals.

- Pair the group and make sure each pair has two pieces of paper and two pencils.
- *Divide one page into four by making a big cross in the middle.*
- *In each square, write a number between 0 and 9.*
- *The other page is for keeping score.*
- *Now, I will say a number. If you have that number written on your page, give yourself a point on the score page.*
- *However, if you can* **make** *that number, by adding/subtracting/dividing/ multiplying* (decides which operation to use depending on class abilities), *then give yourself a point. You and your partner can quickly discuss this possibility.*
- *For example, if you have both the numbers 1 and 3 on your page, and the number called is 4, then you can add 1 and 3 to get 4, so you get a point.*
- *But here's the catch. If you use two or more numbers to get the called-out number, you must write the sum in the square of the first number used in that operation.*

1 + 3+ 7 = 11 1	3 − 1 = 2 3 + 1 = 4 3
0	7 7 − 3 = 4

Scoring
Using addition and subtraction

Number called	Points
2	✓
5	✗
3	✓
11	✓
4	✓✓

24 Written Rumour

Any

Art

English

History & Geography

Maths

PE

PSHE

Science

Objective To write and rewrite a statement, and observe the changes.

- *For this game you will need a pen or pencil each, and one sheet of paper per group.*
- *Each person will read a sentence written by the person before him or her, then will hide that sentence from view by folding the paper.* Demonstrate how to fold the paper horizontally to cover the sentence.
- *Then you will rewrite the sentence so that it means the same thing – or almost the same thing – but you will try to use different words.*
- *For example, if the first sentence says, 'I went to town to buy groceries', the next person could write, 'I went to the shop to buy bread and milk'.*
- *Each person will just have a few seconds to silently read, rewrite and pass it on.*
- *Give the first person in each group the opening sentence, without the others seeing, or they can create their own.*
- *This is a timed game. At the end of 60 seconds, we will read what each group has written as a final sentence.*

Individuals

Partners

Small Group (5–6)

Whole Group

Follow Up Discuss the final sentences, quickly talk about how they have changed and why.

Extended Follow Up This activity lends itself to in-depth discussions of how and why rumours start, gather speed, get corrupted, etc.

Possible Opening Sentences

- The animals in the jungle were in danger of extinction.
- The students ran from the school when the fire alarm went off.
- In my kitchen there are cooking utensils and food.
- My bag is amazing because it hold so many precious items.
- The movie was scary but the popcorn was buttery and good.
- Everyone in our group has good work skills, good manners and a good haircut.
- I have a perfect pet because it is small and cuddly.

25 Shared-Pen Stories

Objective To write a sentence or short story by sharing a single writing tool. Pair the group and provide a single piece of blank paper per pair; consider new ways of forming pairs (not always 'the person next to you').

Note No speaking is allowed.

- *You are going to write a story/sentence together, but you cannot talk about what you are going to write.*
- *I will give you a topic, then partner A will start writing whatever comes to mind.*
- *When I give the signal partner B will take the pen and continue on from where A left off.*
- *Remember – no talking. You just have to guess what your partner might have been going to say.*
- *When a thought is finished, put a full stop after it and continue writing until the signal.*
- Give the signal approximately every ten seconds. (This may need to be adjusted according to the age of the group.)
- *When I tell you to stop, you will read over what you have written together and be ready to read it to the whole group.*

Follow Up *Read your sentence/story to another pair (or the whole group). How good were you at working out what your partner was thinking?*

Write About
• Pet peeves • Sisters or brothers • Homework • Friends

26 Zoom-Out

Any

Art

English

History & Geography

Maths

PE

PSHE

Science

Individuals

Partners

Small Group

Whole Group

Objective To create a picture/illustration that begins with a very tiny detail and works outward.

Notes An excellent resource for this type of thinking is the picture book *Zoom* by Istvan Banyai (available on Amazon).

Pair students and provide a single piece of blank paper per pair.

- *Your job will be to create something that quite naturally starts small and gets larger.*
- *For example, this is sort of like looking first at your fingernail, then gradually at your whole body.*
- *For this activity there can be quiet talking as you and your partner work out what you are drawing. It might take a few moments for you to do this.*
- *In the meantime, you must keep adding to the picture. Maybe nothing will grow out of your picture and it will end up being an abstract or design, and that's OK too.*
- *Partner A, please draw a dot in the centre of the page.*
- *Now partner B, without discussion, add something to the dot. Keep it small.*
- *Now each time I signal you will hand over the pencil and keep taking turns adding something to the drawing, moving from the centre of the page outwards.*
- Signal every ten seconds or so. If anyone is stuck, make suggestions such as *Maybe it could be an eye, a spot on something, a button, a pimple.* Once everyone gets the idea, this task truly catapults.

Follow Up *Were you able to create an actual representation of something? Name your illustration.*

Extended Follow Up *Where in science do we look closely at things like this? Discuss or write about this concept.*

Showcase *Show your illustration to another pair (or the whole class).*

27 Scrabble® Scramble

Objective	To create a crossword puzzle using words related to a theme.

Props	A list of words: these can be themed according to the subject being studied. The number used will depend on the group's age and ability.

- Give each pair a sheet of paper with a grid, such as graph paper; the squares should be sized according to the age and ability of your group.
- *This activity involves you being creative with words and putting them together to form a crossword puzzle – just like playing Scrabble®.*
- *I will give you the list of words. You and your partner need to pick any one you want to begin with, then try to fit in as many of the others as you can.*
- *You will have two minutes* [or more, depending on your purpose] *to see who can fit the most words together.*

```
    P
N   O   U   N   S
    E
    T               E
W   R   I   T   I   N   G
    Y               G
                    L
                    I
                    S
                    H
```

Follow Up	Ask around the group to find out how many words were correctly used. Select winners.

Extended Follow Up	Make further use of the created puzzles by asking the group to write definitions in appropriate crossword style. They can then exchange with other pairs to complete the blank crosswords.

Any (as source of theme)
Art
English
History & Geography
Maths
PE
PSHE
Science

Individuals
Partners
Small Group
Whole Group

28 Add-Ons

Any

Art

English

History & Geography

Maths

PE

PSHE

Science

Objective To create a drawing taking turns adding components. Pair the group and provide each pair with paper and a pencil. Have them decide which partner will be A, and which will be B.

Note No speaking allowed.

- *This game involves careful cooperation with your partner. You will take turns drawing, but each of you only draw a single part of the picture.*
- *For example, if you were drawing a house, partner A might draw the roof, then partner B might add the sides, and so on.*
- *The trick is that you can't talk to each other; you'll have to work out what your partner is trying to draw by watching and imagining.*
- *To start with I will tell you what to draw. A will draw that, then B will draw, and so on.*
- *At the beginning, keep your drawings fairly small so that you can keep adding on to them without running out of space.*
- *Remember – only one part of the drawing per person.*
- Watch that students don't 'keep the pencil' to draw more than a single component at a time. Use the cue approximately every ten seconds to indicate when to change partners.

Individuals

Partners

Small Group

Whole Group

Follow Up Stop drawing and discuss with your partner how well your combined drawing went – or didn't go.

Extended Follow Up You may want to discuss or put on the wall some or all of the results, or follow-up with written reflections.

Possible Starts
- a circle 'face' • a tree • a hat • a bird • a roof with a chimney
- a wheel • a stick man • a wagon • a hand

29 Blind Draw

Objective To try to draw (or write) without looking.

Props Blindfolds, or instruct group members to close their eyes and not look.

- *For this game you will work alone.*
- *In fact, you will be more alone than usual as you will be blindfolded/ keeping your eyes closed.*
- *You job will be to write/draw without looking at your page.*
- *You will start and stop at the signal.*
- *Start by feeling the edges of your page before you put on your blindfold/close your eyes).*
- *I will tell you what to write/draw.*
- *Ready? Begin. Keep writing/drawing until I signal to stop.*

Follow Up *Uncover your eyes and look at your work. How good is it? You can discuss it with a neighbour. Why was it difficult?*

Extended Follow Up You may wish to tie this activity to lessons about differentiation, disabilities or even the concept of having less than others in our society or in the world in general.

30 Snow-Globe Drawings

Any

Art

English

History & Geography

Maths

PE

PSHE

Science

Objective To connect random dots into a reasonable facsimile of a picture.

- *Pair up and decide who is A and who is B.*
- *Partner B, you will think of a snow globe, pretend you are inside one, and draw the snowflakes all over your page. In other words, fill the page with dots.*
- *However, I am going to put a limit on the number of snowflakes in your globe; you have only …* (Choose a number from 20 to 40; use fewer dots for younger groups as the more dots there are, the more difficult the task.)
- *OK, begin. B, make dots anywhere you want on the page.*
- *Now it's A's turn. A, you must find a way to connect these dots to make a picture. And you have to use them all. Maybe your picture will have to be an abstract design.*
- *You have one minute to do this.*
- Get the pairs to swap roles so each has a chance to try each part of this creative activity. Children are much more adept at joining random dots than adults, and you may be surprised at the results.

Individuals

Partners

Small Group

Whole Group

Follow Up Pairs can talk about their pictures with others for a few moments.

Extended Follow Up Invite the pairs to present their pictures to the group if they wish to.

31 Mirror Images

Objective To create symmetrical illustrations or designs.

Note Everyone has looked in a mirror. When you do this, the image you see is actually a reversed or opposite image of yourself.

- *Now one of you will be the mirror.*
- *Begin by folding your paper lengthwise to make a crease, then opening it flat again.*
- *Decide who is A and who is B.*
- *A, you will work on the right side of the crease; B will work on the left.*
- *A, you begin by drawing something simple: an object such as an apple or a flower.* (It may be easier for younger or less able groups to start with single lines – a curved line, a diagonal line – before moving to shapes.)
- *B, you try to reproduce a symmetrical mirror-image, the way it would look in a mirror. Remember details need to be reversed.*
- *Now B, you add something to the image, and A will copy it.*
- *You will continue in this manner until I signal you to stop.*

Any

Art

English

History & Geography

Maths

PE

PSHE

Science

Individuals

Partners

Small Group

Whole Group

Follow Up Look closely at your pages. Is one side exactly symmetrical to the other? How can you check? (Refold on the crease and hold up to the light to see if the lines correspond.)

Extended Follow Up You may wish to discuss problems with this task, or where, in nature or real life, symmetry exists.

3 Up and At 'Em

Get Moving

The 3-Minute Motivators in this section are designed to provide groups with a controlled escape for energy while at the same time energising those who may be bored or sleepy. In most cases groups remain seated, but are involved in innovative, teacher-led, movement-based activities – on their own. They will be involved in a variety of low-risk activities that will challenge them to be creative and focused. Cognition, imagination, short-term memory and fine motor skills all come into play, as well as accurate looking, listening to directions and deciphering non-verbal communication cues.

- Most of these 3-Minute Motivators are individual activities. In some instances, however, the individuals become a part of the whole-class activity (e.g., 'Thunderstorm', page 56).
- Most 'Get Moving' motivators are silent activities and group leaders will need to reinforce this point. Communication may still occur, but it is non-verbal communication. Before beginning the movement, reinforce that this is a silent activity.
- Teachers will probably choose 'Get Moving' refocusers if they want to engage classes actively, yet minimise student interaction. However, whole-class discussions can easily follow any of the activities.

These activities are visible to all and, therefore, can be more entertaining than those in the previous chapter. The magic of these refocusers lies in the reduction of hyperactivity that is fostered by the restricted, seated actions.

32 Open – Shut – Shake

Any (especially where fine motor control is required)

Art

English

History & Geography

Maths

PE

PSHE

Science

Objective To mimic increasingly difficult hand movements.

Note This is a good hand exercise; using it prior to a lengthy writing exercise may be useful.

- *Sit straight in your desk, feet on the floor, eyes on me.*
- *I am going to demonstrate a hand movement that will be either opening/closing hands* [O/C] *or a shake of the hands.* Demonstrate by opening/closing hands once and shaking loose hands twice.
- *Your job is to repeat exactly what I have done.*
- Begin simply: e.g., three shakes, three O/C. Then increase difficulty: e.g., one O/C, two shakes, four O/C, one shake, etc. The increasing difficulty keeps students on their toes.
- Invite group members to take turns being the leader.
- Or invite group members to turn to a partner and come up with an innovative combination of O/C plus shakes – one they can share with the whole group.

Individuals

Partners

Small Group

Whole Group

Showcase Invite students to prepare a demonstration piece.

33 Puppet Master

Objective To experience being controlled by puppet strings.

- *Sit quietly at your desk, feet on floor, arms draped across desk, head on desk.*
- *Close your eyes.*
- *You are going to become a marionette, a puppet on strings.*
- *I am the puppeteer. When I tell you I am pulling a certain string, you must move only that part of your body.*
- *Relax completely. You are a puppet with no bones. Breathe deeply.*
- *Now I am gently pulling your right arm up …*
- *… and down*
- *Your left arm up.* Continue in this manner until all body parts have been gently raised or moved. Be sure to raise unusual parts, such as elbows, wrists, left ear and so on.
- *Now I am going to pull several strings at once and you will sit up – carefully. I haven't lifted your head yet.*
- *Now your head.* Continue as long as desired or until the groups tires.
- *Feel your strange body.*
- *It is being held up only by strings.*
- *Now I am very gently wiggling the strings.*
- *You stay sitting down, but your body moves in tiny wiggles – all over.*
- *Now I'm going to cut the strings and you will all gently drop back to your desk – when I tell you. NOW!*

Any | Art | **English** | **History & Geography** | Maths | PE | PSHE | Science

Individuals | Partners | Small Group | Whole Group

Follow Up Describe to a neighbour what it felt like to be moved by a puppeteer.

34 The Big Yawn

Any

Art

English

History & Geography

Maths

PE

PSHE

Science

Objective To 'fake' yawning and stretching with as much reality as possible.

- *Sit comfortably, feet on floor.*
- *Listen to my voice. You are feeling very tired*
- *You need to yawn. Go ahead – yawn.*
- *Bigger, bigger … keep yawning and watch your neighbours as you yawn.*
- Since yawning is contagious, if the teacher can also yawn (or fake a yawn) this helps. By inviting students to watch others yawn, eventually some will actually be yawning.
- Now encourage further: *Now add stretches to your yawns. Big, huge, long stretches. Stretch every part of you body. Make no noise – just stretch and yawn.*

Individuals

Partners

Small Group

Whole Group

Follow Up This is a good activity to discuss as groups will be interested in the contagious effect of stretching and yawning. Examine how they felt having to follow instructions and perform artificially something that is usually automatic.

Showcase Some group members will *love* sharing their amazing yawn and stretch combinations.

35 Glass Blower

Objective To imagine blowing glass into something beautiful.

Note Remind groups that they are to remain quiet throughout and to concentrate on their own actions.

- *Sit quietly, feet on floor, hands on desk.*
- *You are going to be a glass blower. On your desk there is a lump of soft glass.*
- *Pick it up. Feel it. It's like squishy clay.*
- *Now make your hands into gentle fists and place them to your mouth as if they were a long blowing tube.* Demonstrate: put the thumb side of one loose fist to the mouth and the thumb side of the other behind it to form a hollow 'tube'.
- *Your lump of glass is attached to the end of your tube. Now you are going to blow gently through your hands and the glass will start to take form. Blow gently; if you blow too hard, you will destroy the glass.*
- *Concentrate on what you are making with your glass. Are you making a vase? A glass animal? A beautiful ornament? A crystal ball? Look at it as you blow – slowly – carefully.*
- Keep coaching them like this for 30 to 60 seconds.
- *Now your item is complete. You will very carefully put your tube down by releasing your hands and gently remove the object from the end. Careful. It's warm; it's very delicate.*
- *Put it on your desk and look at it. Isn't it beautiful?*
- *Look at all the detail.*
- *Memorise what it looks like.*
- *You made this by being calm and gentle.*

Any

Art

English

History & Geography

Maths

PE

PSHE

Science

Individuals

Partners

Small Group

Whole Group

Showcase Group members, in turn, can quickly tell the group what they have 'created'.

36 Levitating Arms

Any

Art

English

History & Geography

Maths

PE

PSHE

Science

Objective To experience the unusual feeling of arms raising on their own.

- *Sit tall, hands on desktops, feet flat on floor.*
- *You are going to spread your arms a little wider than your shoulders and press your hands firmly down to the tops of the desks.* Demonstrate this on your own desk; press the entire palm down.
- *Now you try. Keep pushing until I say stop.* Wait for 60 seconds; continually encourage them to keep pushing.
- *When I tell you to stop, just let your arms float into the air. STOP!* Demonstrate floating your arms.
- *What happened? How do your arms feel?* They will feel light, almost weightless, depending on how much pressure was exerted and for how long the pressure was held.
- *Now we'll try it another way. Put the palm of one hand on the back of the other. Push up with the bottom hand and down with the top one. Hold the pressure until I tell you to stop.* Continue up to 60 seconds.
- *Let go and let the bottom hand rise up. Is it the same feeling?*

Individuals

Partners

Small Group

Whole Group

Follow Up It is important to allow a few minutes to discuss probable reasons for this strange feeling. Ask the group what the experience felt like and why they thought it felt this way. This is a very brief motivator and a quick debriefing can easily fit within the three-minute time frame.

Extended Follow Up A good extension for this motivator is a descriptive writing task.

37 Life Rhythms

Objective To connect speed of tapping with different life emotions.

- *Sit straight in your desk, feet on the floor, eyes on me.*
- *We are going to tap our desks with fingers/clap our hands either very slowly, a little faster or very quickly, depending on the signals I give you.* Demonstrate very slow taps, then very quick taps.
- *Some feelings or emotions feel like they slow us down – like fear, for instance. It might tap slowly.* Demonstrate and let the group copy. *But excitement would be very fast.* Demonstrate and let the group copy.
- *Some feelings might be very soft taps, while others might be hard taps. It's up to you to choose. I might choose soft and slow for a feeling like worry.*
- *Now I will name an emotion and you will tap the speed you think best describes that feeling. This is not a competition – everyone might tap different speeds and that's okay. Just tap for yourself and keep the speed you choose until I call out a different emotion.*

Any
Art
English
History & Geography
Maths
PE
PSHE
Science

Individuals
Partners
Small Group
Whole Group

Follow Up It might be a good idea to briefly discuss the correlation between the rhythms the group tapped and the rhythm of their hearts. This could lead to a lesson on how we handle emotions and, therefore, protect our hearts.

38 Thunderstorm

Any

Art

English

History & Geography

Maths

PE

PSHE

Science

Objective To create the sounds of a storm using the hands and feet.

- *Sit straight in your desk, feet on the floor, eyes on me.*
- *We are going to create a thunderstorm right here in the class.*
- *Begin by rubbing your palms together.* Continue for about 10 seconds. *This is the wind.*
- *Now change to finger snapping.* Continue for about 10 seconds. *The rain.*
- *Now clap – the rain getting harder*
- *Keep clapping and add feet stamping – harder rain and thunder. Harder! HARDER!*
- Continue for no more than 20 seconds, then reverse the sequence.
- *Thunder has stopped!*
- *Rain is stopping. Gentle rain.* Snapping gets slower and lighter.
- *Wind turns to breeze.* Progress from quickly rubbing hands together to slowly rubbing and eventually stopping.
- *Listen to the silence following the storm.* Allow 30 seconds of silent listening.

Individuals (as part of Whole Group)

Partners

Small Group

Whole Group

39 Cold – Hot – Not

Objective To make instant decisions about whether something is cold, hot or neither.

- *This is a fast-thinking game. If I call out something, like 'ice', that is cold, you shout 'COLD!'.*
- *If I call something like 'fire', you shout 'HOT!'.*
- *If I call something like 'coffee' that can be either, you shout 'NOT!'.*
- *You have to pay close attention and think quickly.*
- Remind the group that not everyone will respond in the same way and that's okay. *'Hot' and 'Cold' can also be used to describe likes and dislikes, for example, for the word 'opera', I might respond 'Hot!' if I like opera, while some people might respond 'Cold!' if they don't like it.*
- With younger children, use concrete words. With older children, increase the difficulty by using more abstract words and explaining that their responses depend on how they feel about the item or situation.

Concrete Words

- Winter, fall, spring, summer, sun, moon
- Niagara Falls, Pacific Ocean, Arctic Sea
- Sauna, shower, swimming pool, bath
- Food & drink, e.g., ice cream, spaghetti, soup, hot chocolate
- Campfire, candle flame, oven, freezer
- Steam, smoke, tornado, hurricane

Abstract Concepts

- Homework, housework
- School subjects
- Friends, enemies, family, relatives, teachers, sports coaches
- Types of music; e.g., rap, hip-hop, classical, country, rock, pop
- Current TV shows or films
- Current TV or film stars, athletes, famous people
- Clothing fads or brands; e.g., Adidas, Nike
- Popular fast food; e.g., hamburgers, pizza, milkshakes
- Familiar activities; e.g., going to the cinema, going skating, talking on the phone
- Popular technology; e.g., MP3 player, camera mobile phone
- Hairstyles; e.g., ponytail, crew-cut, brightly coloured hair, Mohican; dreadlocks, shaved head

Any (as source of words)
Art
English
History & Geography
Maths
PE
PSHE
Science

Individuals (as part of Whole Group)
Partners
Small Group
Whole Group

40 Stuck!

Any
Art
English
History & Geography
Maths
PE
PSHE
Science

Individuals
Partners
Small Group
Whole Group

Objective To experience being 'stuck' to the desk.

- *Sit comfortably at your desk, feet on the floor.*
- *Stretch your arms across the desk and put your head down on the desk.*
- *Get as comfortable as possible, with as much of your body touching the desktop as possible.*
- *Listen carefully. When I give you the signal, you are suddenly going to be completely stuck to your desk.*
- *Your feet will be stuck to the floor.*
- *You will need to listen for my signals before you'll be able to get unstuck.*
- Signal. *You are totally stuck. You can't lift anything.*
- *Try to lift your head. Impossible!*
- *Try each arm – stuck fast!*
- *For the next few seconds you will try unsuccessfully to lift different parts of your body, but you are too tightly stuck.* Wait for about 15 seconds. If anyone succeeds in 'lifting' a body part, just remind them all that they should be too stuck to move.
- *Feel the heaviness of your head stuck to the desk.*
- *Feel the weight of your arms … hands … legs. You might be able to move your knees, but your feet don't move at all.*
- Continue in this manner for up to two minutes.
- *The glue is starting to weaken. You can lift one hand … one arm …*
- Continue giving 'unstuck' cues until everyone is sitting upright again.
- *One final thing is stuck – your backside. You are stuck to your seat and will stay that way until the end of the lesson!*

Follow Up Ask how many people actually had a sense of being stuck. You may wish to discuss possible reason for this.

41 False Freeze

Objective	To stand up or sit down according to whether or not what the leader says is true; to 'freeze' if a statement is false.

Props	True/False sentences from any subject area. These can be made up on the spot or chosen from a previously prepared bank of statements.

- *Sit sideways in your chair so that you can stand up easily and quickly without bumping anyone else.*
- *You are going to stand up, sit down or freeze every time I say something.*
- *If I say something that is true, like 'I am your group leader' and you are sitting down, you must stand up quickly. True statements require you to move, to change position.*
- *If next I say something false, like 'I am a car', you must freeze. In other words, stay standing or sitting, don't move at all. False statements require you to freeze.*
- *Then, if I say, 'You are students' – that's true – you can move again and sit back down.*
- *So you **move** every time I say something true. If I say something false, you **freeze** where you are.*
- Provide sentences slowly at first; gradually increase speed so that everyone is really moving. This sounds easier than it is. Kids love it and teachers can use this exercise to revise basic subject concepts.

Extended Follow Up	Statements with 'debatable' or 'sometimes' responses can lead to effective discussions and writing tasks.

True-False

- Boys are usually taller than girls.
- Ice melts when heated.
- The sky can be orange.
- Birds fly.
- Dogs meow.
- Chocolate is always brown.
- Blueberries are purple.
- Apple sauce is made from pears.
- Erasers remove ink
- Cows drink milk.
- Coffee is always hot.
- A pencil is made of wood.
- Teachers are always female.
- The gym is used for assemblies.
- Ink is blue.
- Mobile phones hurt your eyes.
- Video games are always good for you.

Any
Art
English
History & Geography
Maths
PE
PSHE
Science

Individuals
Partners
Small Group
Whole Group

41 False Freeze *continued*

Any
Art
English
History & Geography
Maths
PE
PSHE
Science

Another way to use False Freeze is with rhyming (move) and non-rhyming (freeze) words.

Rhyming	Non-Rhyming
See, be, tree, he, free, knee	See, saw
Look, cook, book, nook, took	Tree, trunk
May, hay, stay, OK, yay	Lay, lie
Run, sun, gun, fun, begun, done	Call, hail
Rain, pain, vein, train	Rub, tarp
Fool, school, rule, cool, tool	What, where
Caught, ought, taught	Catch, call
You, do, to, blue, shoe, flew	Bird, wing
Green, seen, been, sheen, keen	Cook, cake
Yet, pet, net, get, met, set, let	Mum, dad
Friend, end, send, lend, depend	Note, nice
Girl, pearl, swirl, twirl	Girl, all
Boy, toy, joy, annoy, ploy	Boy, ball
Pick, stick, nick, quick, sick, picnic	Ill, ail
Teeth, beneath, wreath	Tooth, tough
Ape, gape, grape, tape	Fruit, freckle
Late, gate, plate, date, debate	Dad, bag
Grab, crab, lab, dab, flab, nab	Bought, bring
Ring, sing, bring, thing	Song, sing

Individuals
Partners
Small Group
Whole Group

42 Heads or Tails

Objective To select Heads or Tails ten times and record your luck at guessing.

Props A coin, pencil & paper

- *On your paper, write the numbers 1 to 10, in a vertical column.*
- *Now choose Heads or Tails ten times; write 'H' or 'T' beside each number.*
- *I will toss the coin and you will check your guesses.*
- *If you have 'Heads' written beside the number, you must stand up **before** I toss the coin. This way we'll all know who guessed correctly for each toss of the coin.*
- *Stand if you have 'Heads' beside number one.* Toss the coin; tell those who have the correct 'H' or 'T' to give themselves a tick beside that number.
- Continue for all ten numbers, then check for winners; i.e., who has guessed correctly the most times. If too many are winners the first time through, play the winners off against each other and invite the non-players to take turns tossing the coin.

Any

Art

English

History & Geography

Maths (probability)

PE

PSHE

Science

Individuals

Partners

Small Group

Whole Group

43 Ice Cube

Any

Art

English

History & Geography

Maths

PE

PSHE

Science

Objective To experience (in the imagination) the feeling of having an ice cube dropped down your back.

- *Sit tall at your desk, feet on the floor, eyes on me.*
- *Something is going to happen to you – but in your imagination, in your mind. It may be something that has already happened to some of you.*
- *When I give the signal, a big, cold, ice cube will be dropped down your back.*
- *You won't be able to sit still – you'll have to wriggle or do whatever you can to get it out.*
- *But you won't be able to get it out until I give the Stop signal. At that time, the ice cube will be completely melted.*
- *You might need to stand up, but you can't leave your desk area.*
- Signal to start; continue guiding for up to a minute.

Individuals

Partners

Small Group

Whole Group

Follow Up *Could you really* feel *the ice melting in your shirt? What did it feel like? Tell a neighbour.*

Showcase If any person was particularly interesting or amusing, invite them to demonstrate for the whole group.

44 Number Shakes

Objective To achieve a specific number by shaking fists and extending fingers.

Notes No talking is allowed.
This gets a bit competitive, as pairs all want to be the first to get the number. You can play this up or not, depending on your group. It's usually a good idea to stop when several pairs get the number, then start again with a new number. Bigger numbers can involve using all four hands.

- *Turn to face your partner/your neighbour/the person behind you.*
- *Sit comfortably with your feet on the floor.*
- *This is like the game Rock, Paper, Scissors. You shake your fists three times and, on the fourth time, you both open your hands at the same time. But instead of making the sign for rock, paper or scissors, you will hold out as many fingers as you want.*
- *I will call out a number and the goal is for each pair to try to shake the number I call.*
- *For example, if I call 3, then one partner would need one finger and the other would need two.*
- *Or one partner might shake no fingers (that is, keep the fist closed), while the partner puts out three.*
- *Keep track of how many tries you and your partner need to reach the magic number. As soon as you get the number, raise your hands.*

Follow Up To increase the level of difficulty for older groups, try positive and negative integers. One partner is positive, the other negative; they must come up with the called number. Or use with subtraction (subtract one number from another to get the called number), multiplication or even division. Lots of variables are possible.

Another alternative is to challenge two or more group members to shake exactly the same number. In other words, how many tries does it take for both to shake, for example, a three?

Any
Art
English
History & Geography
Maths
PE
PSHE
Science

Individuals
Partners
Small Group
Whole Group

45 Lucky Hi/Lo

Any

Art

English

History & Geography

Maths

PE

PSHE

Science

Objective To test luck by trying to match the high or low called by the teacher.

This is like 'Number Shakes' (page 63) in that it follows the Rock, Paper, Scissors process of shaking closed fists three times and opening on the fourth shake.

Props Pencil & paper

Notes No speaking allowed.

- *Begin by writing your name and your partner's name side by side on a piece of paper. Use a little part of your workbook if you like.*
- *Sit facing your partner, feet on the floor.*
- *Make fists and shake three times. On the fourth shake you will open your fists to hold out any number of fingers out you choose.* Allow a couple of practices.
- *Now comes the game part. After you open your fists, I will be calling 'High' or 'Low'. The person whose fingers match what I call gets a point under his or her name.* Demonstrate by using both of your hands. Hold up one finger on one hand and three on the other and demonstrate which hand is high and which is low.
- *If you both show the same number, neither of you gets the point.*
- *To make it fair, I won't watch you as you open your fists.* Turn away but count 'One, two, three' with the group, then say either 'High' or 'Low'. Make the calling random. Avoid just alternating, as groups will be quick to pick up on this.

Individuals

Partners

Small Group

Whole Group

46 Monkey See, Monkey Do

Objective To create a sequence of interesting arm and hand movements.

Note No speaking allowed.

- *Turn to face your partner.*
- *Sit straight in your chairs, feet on floor, arms resting on desktops.*
- *Decide who is A and who is B.*
- *Partner A will make an arm or hand movement, something simple like this.* Demonstrate opening and closing hands twice quickly.
- *Partner B will copy the movement, then add another movement, like this.* Demonstrate opening/closing hands twice, then quietly clapping three times.
- *You will keep taking turns adding movements until I give you the Stop signal.*
- *Try to remember all the actions in sequence. After the Stop signal, you and your partner will go through the whole sequence together.*
- *This is a silent activity; no talking, just doing.*

Any that use sequencing skills

Art

English

History & Geography

Maths

PE

PSHE

Science

Individuals

Partners

Small Group

Whole Group

Showcase This is an activity groups love to show off. Allow a few pairs (as many as time allows) to demonstrate their complete sequence in unison.

Possible Movements

- Snap fingers
- Use imaginary lassos
- Tap knuckles together
- Tap desks, knees, forehead, ears
- Shake index fingers
- Make punching movements

47 Musical Punching Bags

Any

Art

English

History & Geography

Maths

PE

PSHE

Science

Objective To punch imaginary punching bags and attach tones to the punches.

Note This is not a silent activity, as it involves students making musical tones. However, these sounds can be omitted entirely and the activity will still be effective.

- *Turn to your partner.*
- *Sit with your feet on the floor, facing each other. Make fists*
- *Imagine a small punching bag. It is hanging right in front of you, but not close to your partner.*
- *Take a few practice punches in the air. Remember to stay out of your partner's punching area.*
- *You and your partner are going to take turns punching a bag that hangs between you. It's a small punching bag but, each time you punch it, the bag makes a musical noise of some sort. Remember it's a small bag, so it's a small noise.* It's a good idea for the teacher to demonstrate a couple of musical punches here.
- *Take turns with the bag. Try to be creative.* Give the signal to start.
- Wait about 30 to 40 seconds. *Now take turns copying what your partner did, then adding to that, until you have an interesting combination of punches and sounds.*
- *Pay attention to the most interesting punch-noise combinations you and your partner can come up with. You might be able to show everyone these later.*

Individuals

Partners

Small Group

Whole Group

Showcase Invite some pairs to demonstrate their punch-sound combinations.

48 Magic Mirrors

Objective	To create a mirror image of the slow, smooth actions of a partner.
Props	Slow, moving music without words; the activity can also be done without music.
Note	No speaking allowed.

- *Turn to face your partner (your neighbour, the person in front of you) and sit up straight with your feet on the floor.*
- *Your job will be to mirror each other's actions. Whatever your partner does with his or her hands and arms, you do exactly the same.*
- *But remember that a mirror shows the opposite, so if your partner is leading and he or she pulls back, you pull back too.* Demonstrate with a group member.
- *Try to be creative. Make big but very slow movements.*
- *You must maintain eye contact! That's the trick here. Don't look at your partner's hands; look only at the eyes. So MOVE SLOWLY!*
- *If you are the leading partner, you are not trying to trick your partner. You are trying to lead and be followed exactly.*
- *Decide who will be the first leader. Start when the music begins. When I give the signal, change leaders.*
- Give the start signal.
- Allow about 30 seconds, then give the signal to change leaders.

Showcase	This activity lends itself to pairs quickly demonstrating a sequence of movements with the class; don't push anyone to demonstrate if they are not keen to do so.

49 Tap It to Me

Any

Art

English

History & Geography

Maths

PE

PSHE

Science

Objective To work out words by spelling them onto a partner's palm.

Props Pencil & paper

Note No speaking allowed. Difficulty can be determined by your choice of words. It can also be increased by writing a complete short sentence rather than single words.

- *This is a challenge game. You and your partner will challenge the other pairs.*
- *I will give you a word, but only one person in each pair will see it.*
- *That partner will spell it into the palm of the other partner's hand by tapping the correct number of times for each letter's place in the alphabet.*
- *For example, if the word was* cat, *I'd first tap three times, because 'C' is the third letter of the alphabet. My partner would write down the letter 'C'.*
- *As soon as my partner writes the letter 'C', I go on the next letter. I tap once for 'A'.*
- *My partner writes 'A'.*
- *If my partner guesses the word based on these two letters, he or she can write the whole word. If it's correct, I can go on to the next word and continue until we have all the words.*
- *If my partner makes a mistake, I shake my head. Remember – no talking!*
- *I will put the words on the board* [Choose from two to five words.], *so one partner has to turn now so as not to see the board.*
- *If your partner loses track or you tap the wrong number, moving your hands side-to-side* [Demonstrate] *lets the other person know to start again.*
- Signal to start. Stop when the first pair indicates completion of all words.

Individuals

Partners

Small Group

Whole Group

50 Shake It!

Objective	To alternate between moving silently and stealthily and shaking the entire body vigorously at a signal.

Note	It is inevitable that, with many people moving at the same time, they will need to be reminded not to infringe on others. The idea of a personal-space bubble is one many group leaders use. It refers to the imaginary sphere that surrounds and encapsulates every group member. Appreciation of the 'bubbles' of peers seems to be a concept readily understood and accepted by children of all ages.

- *This game is fun because you get to shake your entire body – just like a dog might shake when it's wet.*
- *But you can only shake everything when I say 'Shake it!'*
- *The rest of the time, you will shake only the body part I call out.*
- *When I give the Start signal, please stand and walk carefully around the room, being careful of everyone else's space; stay out of each other's 'bubbles'.*
- Signal to begin. Alternate different body parts with 'Shake it!'

Any

Art

English

History & Geography

Maths

PE

PSHE

Science

Individuals

Partners

Small Group

Whole Group

Body Parts

• fingers • head • hands • nose • shoulders • hair
• one foot (leg, arm, knee, elbow) • backside

Act, Don't Speak

The 3-Minute Motivators in this section require moderate physical involvement on the part of the students. The activities will require them to stand beside or behind their desks and move in some fanciful manner, either alone or with others (i.e., in partners or small groups). In some cases they will actually move around the room. However, these are silent refocusers; no talking is allowed; this helps to control any heightened energy that may accompany the activities. The very nature of these motivators makes them excellent for very active groups who need to burn off a bit of energy before more focused seated sessions or a listening activity. Older groups still benefit from getting up and moving when they start to feel or act bored or sleepy.

Because the group members are acting or doing, they are, in fact, representing. They are also listening closely to signals from the leader. Short-term memory and imagination, as well as thinking skills, come into play as groups engage in the various activities. If showcasing is involved, instant visualisation is added to the repertoire of areas being addressed.

Note

- Most groups enjoy these more active exploits. However, if someone is shy, challenged in any way or just feeling 'out of it', it's a good idea to promote the use of the Pass – the right to 'sit this one out as long as you refocus with everyone else when it's over'.
- Remember to reinforce the silent nature of these activities; often the fun is greater simply because no *verbal* communication is allowed.

51 Fast Feet

Any

Art

English

History & Geography

Maths

PE

PSHE

Science

Objective	To provide an escape for excess energy by quickly, silently 'running' feet.

- *Stand quietly beside your desk. Remember to stay in your own space bubble.*
- *When I give the Start signal, you will quickly and quietly run on the spot. You will move your feet as fast as possible for five seconds. Then, on the signal, stop the fast feet and change to slow, silent marching on the spot.*
- *During the fast-feet times, bend over slightly.*
- *During the slow-march times, stand as tall as possible.*
- Continue alternating fast feet/slow march – five seconds each, for up to two minutes. Demonstrate, if necessary, how to move feet very quickly without noise or forward movement.

Individuals

Partners

Small Group

Whole Group

52 Melt

Objective To melt into nothing, as a candle or snowman would.

- *Stand beside your desk.*
- *Stand as tall as possible. You are a snowman/candle.*
- *When I give the Start signal, you will start to melt. Remember to melt from the top down – very, very slowly.*
- *See if you can take a full 60 seconds to melt into a puddle on the floor. I will tell you as the time passes.*
- Signal to start.
- Call out when each 10 seconds has passed.
- Once they are on the floor, say, *Now you are just a puddle of water/wax. Relax. Don't move. When I give the signal you will return to sitting at your desk.*

Any

Art

English

History & Geography

Maths

PE

PSHE

Science

Individuals

Partners

Small Group

Whole Group

Follow Up *What did it feel like? Discuss with a neighbour.*

Showcase If any one was particularly interesting, invite them to show the group their 'melt'.

53 Balancing Act

Any

Art

English

History & Geography

Maths

PE

PSHE

Science

Objective To balance in various positions.

- *For this game you will need to stand quietly beside your desks.*
- *I will ask you to balance in some different ways.*
- *Listen carefully and hold the balance once you get it.*
- *A good tip is to look at a spot on the floor about one body-length in front of you. Focus on that imaginary spot and it will be easier to keep your balance.*
- *You will be competing with yourself; try to increase the time you can hold a position each time we do it.*
- *If you lose your balance, take a breath and re-balance*
- Increase the time to hold each balance, beginning with 15 seconds and working up to 60 seconds.
- Challenge the group to come up with other balance poses.

Use your judgment as to the difficulty of the balances you ask the group to attempt. The following balances are listed in order of difficulty, from easiest to most challenging:

1 Simple Stork: one leg on other knee; arms out to sides

2 Complex Stork: one leg on knee; hands clasped above head

3 Simple Skater: one leg extended behind; arms to sides

4 Harder Skater: one leg extended behind; arms pushed out in front, hands clasped

5 Complex Skater: one leg extended behind; arms tightly presses to sides

6 Simple Pretzel: one leg behind, foot held with opposite hand (i.e., right hand holds left foot); other arm out straight

7 Complex Pretzel: Same as Simple Pretzel, but with other arm behind back

8 Easy Squat: Squat down with one leg extended in front, arms wide

9 Complex Squat: Same as Easy Squat but with arms behind back

Individuals

Partners

Small Group

Whole Group

54 Bump on the Head

Objective To be a nail or a screw and experience being hammered or screwed into a piece of wood.

- *Stand quietly beside your desk.*
- *When I give the Start signal, you will become a huge nail/screw.*
- *Then every time I give the signal a huge hammer/screwdriver will hit you on the head/turn you and push you a little further into the ground.*
- *Remember that your feet will be the first to disappear, then a little more with each bang.*
- *You'll end up squatting as close to the floor as possible. It will take about ten hits /turns for this.*

Knocking Knees

Any

Art

English

History & Geography

Music

PE

PSHE

Science

Objective To maintain a continually expanding sequence of clap/knee actions.

- *For this game you must turn sideways in your chairs.*
- *We are going to keep a rhythm using just our hands and knees.*
- *I'll start you off.*
- *Then I'll call out a name and that person will add another movement to the sequence. We'll keep building until we can't remember anymore.*
- *If I call your name and you can't think of anything, just say 'Pass'.*
- *Let's start with this:* Clap hands once, slap your knees twice.
- Repeat this sequence a few times before calling the first person to follow.

Individuals (as part of Whole Group)

Partners

Small Group

Whole Group

Suggested Movements

- Bump knees together two or three times
- Click fingers and lift knees alternately
- Open and shut knees several times
- Clap hands on or under knees
- Stamp feet: stamp in/out/in/out, front/back, etc.
- Slap opposite knees; i.e. right hand to left knee, left hand to right knee
- Clap to the side, above, behind backs, far out in front

56 Wide – Hide

Objective To move rapidly from a standing, wide stance to a curled-up, hiding position.

- *First we will stand beside the desks and try to take up as much room as possible without moving.*
- *Spread your arms; stand wide like you are hugging a huge ball.*
- *Now, quickly go from that 'Wide' position – a hugging or welcoming position – to becoming as small as you can, all curled up as if trying to disappear. This is your 'Hide' position.*
- *Now sit normally. I will say something.*
- *If it's something you like or feel good about, immediately become 'Wide' and hug.*
- *If it's something you dislike, or feel bad about or are afraid of, quickly get into the 'Hide' position and try to be invisible.*
- *There can be no in-between. You have to choose either 'Wide' or 'Hide'.*
- *Remember that everyone will have different reactions. There is no right or wrong answer to any of the suggestions. You may want to hide from all of them or you may want to get huge and embrace all of them.*

Suggested Words

- Freezing weather
- Warm sandy beach
- Amusement park
- Pollution
- Foul-smelling rubbish tip
- Rocket to space
- Boys/Girls
- Homework
- Ice-cream sundaes
- Brussel sprouts
- Pizza
- Dancing
- Mountain climbing
- Deep-sea diving
- Going to the dentist
- Monster (horror) films

57 Morphing Madness

Any

Art

English

History & Geography

Maths

PE

PSHE

Science

Objective To work with a partner to quietly create, using only bodies, whatever object or animal the leader calls out.

Note No speaking allowed.

- *You and your partner will need to stand together beside your desks, so make sure you have room to move.*
- *This game requires the two of you to use your bodies to make or represent a single object or animal.*
- *For example, if I call out 'lamp post', one of you might stand tall while the other stands facing with arms straight out.*
- *Or you might stand back to back, both of you with arms out to the side.*
- *Try it.*
- After each body morph, ask everyone to stay in position but to look around at the rest of the group.

Individuals

Partners

Small Group

Whole Group

Showcase Invite any pairs who were particularly creative to demonstrate a specific morph with the class.

Suggested Morphs

- Bridge, tower, house, door, gate, fence, church
- Elephant, giraffe, frog, turtle, alligator, bird, butterfly
- Beach ball, swing, kite, scissors, footstool, ladder, bath, box
- Rock, tree, waterfall

58 Do This! Do That!

Objective To copy only the actions accompanied by the call 'Do this': this is an elimination game.

Note This game is based on 'Simon Says'. It is popular with all ages and its effect is definitely enhanced with prizes.

- *Everyone stand up, please.*
- *When I perform an action and say 'Do this!' you* ***must*** *copy the action.*
- *If I perform an action and say 'Do that!' you* ***must not*** *copy me. In fact, if you move even a tiny bit, you will be out and have to sit down.*
- *The last few people standing will be the winners.*
- *If you are out early, your job is to carefully watch the standing people for any hints of movement on the 'Do that's.*
- Do a practice run. It may be a good idea, if necessary, to stand on a chair so that everyone can easily see you as you lead.
- There will probably be time to play more than once in the three-minute time. To add variety, invite different group members to lead.

59 As the Circle Turns

Any

Art

English

History & Geography

Maths

PE

PSHE

Science

Objective To move left, right, in or out while being part of a circle.

Note No speaking allowed. The idea is to keep the group moving as quickly as possible without endangering anyone. Use your judgment as you see how students behave.

- Begin by getting everyone into either one large group circle holding hands (depending on available room) or several smaller circles (no less than four or five per group) in a part of the room where they can move the circle in either direction.
- Make sure they are standing holding hands.
- *This is a game that will involve cooperation but no talking.*
- *I will give you movement instructions to follow as a group.*
- *For example, I might say, 'Two steps to the right' and you'd have to do that as a group.*
- *At first I will give the instructions slowly, but they will get faster and faster, so you'll need to listen carefully and work together.*
- *No pushing – just cooperating.*

Individuals (as part of Whole Group)

Partners

Small Group

Whole Group

Suggested Movement Instructions

- Any number of lateral steps to either side
- Any number of steps in or out
- Arm movements, such as 'Arms up', 'Arms in', 'Arms down'
- Foot movements, such as 'Left foot off the floor', 'Right leg shake in the air'
- Height instructions, such as 'squat as low as possible', 'stand on tiptoes'

60 Lean on Me

Objective To provide and receive physical support for/from other group members.

- *This is a game of trust and cooperation.*
- *I will give instructions from which you will have to figure out different positions with your partner.*
- *One partner must always be leaning on, or using the other for support.*
- *For example, if I say, 'Back to back', you will stand back to back, but one partner must lean back against the other for support.*
- *You can talk quietly about it as you find the positions, then hold the position until give another instruction.*
- *You must take turns being the one who is supported.*

Any
Art
English
History & Geography
Maths
PE
PSHE
Science

Follow Up Quickly discuss what it felt like to be supported by someone else.

Extended Follow Up Get the group to write or talk metaphorically about being supported.

Showcase Invite pairs to demonstrate a few of the more original poses.

Suggested Position Cues

- Side to side
- Back to side
- Hand to shoulder
- Hand to hand
- One leg off the floor (for one partner)
- Foot to hand
- Knee to knee

Individuals
Partners
Small Group
Whole Group

61 Lump of Clay

Any

Art

English

History & Geography

Maths

PE

PSHE

Science

Objective To take turns moulding partners into different shapes.

Note No speaking is allowed. You can give specific instructions, or the pairs can think of their own ideas.

- *Please stand beside your desk with your partner. Decide who is A and who is B.*
- *When I give the start signal, Partner B will become a very soft lump of clay and Partner A will become the artist who is going to mould that clay.*
- *Partner B, you must allow A to move your body in any way he or she wants to; Partner A, you must protect your clay from hurt or harm, so be careful.*
- *Remember that clay can't talk, so this will be done in silence.*
- *I will know you have created your final piece when A sits down to admire the beautiful sculpture.*
- *I will give you only about two minutes to create your work.*
- Give the Start signal.
- After about two minutes, give the Stop signal.
- If time permits, allow pairs to change roles and repeat the experience.

Individuals

Partners

Small Group

Whole Group

Showcase Invite everyone to look around at what others have sculpted.

Suggested Subjects

- a piece of furniture
- a plant or tree
- an animal
- a telegraph pole

62 Ages of Humanity

Objective To physically experience the rapid aging of a human being.

- *For this game, you and your partner will be two friends who start out life as babies and quickly 'fast forward' to become old people.*
- *You will need to listen carefully to my instructions so you know what to do.*
- *Try to work together to really* feel *what happens to yourselves as you get older and older.*
- *You may use the area beside your desks, but do not interfere with the areas of others. Remember to respect the spaces bubbles of other pairs.*
- *Every time you hear my signal, you will grow older. Listen carefully for the signal and freeze for a few seconds to hear the next directions.*
- *When I signal you to begin, you are both babies in cots that are next to each other. You will have to lie on the floor to do this.*
- Signal to start. Continue at regular intervals with the following (or similar) prompts, remembering to signal between ages.
- *Look at each other. Kick your feet like babies and communicate with each other as babies in cots might do.*
- *Now you are crawling on your hands and knees; you are starting to talk.*
- *Now you are just starting to walk. Lean on each other; take baby steps – remember, stay in your space bubbles.*
- *Now you are four years old, in nursery school. Perhaps you argue over a toy, perhaps you will share.*
- *Now you are ten-year-olds. What are you talking about? How do you behave? You are best friends.*
- *Now you are teenagers. How do you look? Move? Talk? Carry on a conversation like typical teens.*
- *Now you are young adults, still good friends. You have chosen careers – perhaps the same, perhaps different. Discuss your jobs with each other. You are tall, confident, strong.*

Ages of Humanity *continued*

- *Now you are middle-aged – feeling a bit tired. What do you talk about? How do you walk? Are you a bit overweight? Are you overworked? How do you feel? Discuss it together.*
- *Now you are very old, a grandparent. You use a walking stick. You can't see or hear as well as before. Talk together. What do you talk about?*
- *Finally, your ages of humanity are over. When I signal, you will die peacefully by returning to the floor.*

Follow Up	Quickly discuss how it felt to fast-forward the aging process.
Extended Follow Up	Extended whole group discussion and/or a writing project.
Showcase	Invite individuals to demonstrate a specific age.

Words & Movement

The 3-Minute Motivators in this section involve dynamic movements, often away from the desks, as well as verbal interactions. They turn group members into controlled 'movers and shakers'. They all involve everyone working together; none are done on an individual basis.

At first glance it may seem as if these refocusers might be counter-productive, that they might create chaos rather than reduce it. This is not the case. Because the group leader is in control of the activity and because actions are completely structured and directed, the ultimate goals of removing excess energy and/or reducing boredom are magically met.

In these activities, many strands of the English curriculum are covered, often in a single activity. Students are engaged in moving, demonstrating, listening, observing, copying, speaking and, at times, reading and writing. These 3-Minute Motivators tend to make the best activities for introducing lessons.

Groups need to be reminded about personal space, respect for others and safety issues. The following quick rules work well.

- Stay in your own bubble.
- Watch out for others and don't puncture anyone else's bubble.
- Appreciate and respect what everyone is doing. There are no rights or wrongs.
- Be aware of classroom furniture and obstacles. Move with caution.

63 Move It

Any

Art

English

History & Geography

Maths

PE

PSHE

Science

Objective To return to starting positions by moving according to the group leader's directions.

- *First, when I give you the signal to move, you will all walk as far away from your desks as possible and then stand still. Remember to respect each other's personal spaces.*
- Signal to move away from desks/starting positions.
- *Now you will return to your desks in an unusual manner. Wait for the Start signal. Remember each other's spaces.*
- *Follow the 'Move It' instructions as closely as possible.*
- *You can make any sounds you like to accompany the movements, but you cannot use actual words – just sounds.*
- If the group are still restless, repeat the sequence, using a different 'Move It' style.

Individuals

Partners

Small Group

Whole Group

Showcase If someone comes up with a particularly creative move, suggest they demonstrate it for the whole group to enjoy.

Move It Suggestions

- Like a spider, kangaroo, monster, snake, rabbit
- Through a thick jungle, forest, swamp, rushing river
- On slippery ice, broken glass, hot cinders, rocky slope, deep snow
- Backwards
- As if you are very old, are injured, have a broken leg
- Joined to someone else: back to back, hip to hip, elbow to elbow
- Leading with your shoulder, elbow, head, bottom

64 Walk This Way

Objective To duplicate the walk and sound made by a leading partner and to keep changing 'leaders'.

- *Turn to your partner/neighbour/friend.*
- *When I give the Start signal, the two of you will stand, one in front of the other.*
- *When I give the signal again, the front person will start to walk and make a funny but not-too-loud sound.* Demonstrate a march or shuffle accompanied by a soft squeak with each step.
- *The person behind must copy the person in front.*
- *The two of you must keep moving like that until you hear the signal again.*
- *At the signal, both turn around and reverse positions. Now the other person is the leader, creating a different walk and sound.*
- *You must change leaders every time you hear the signal.*
- *You can move anywhere in the room, as long as you respect the personal spaces/bubbles of others.*
- *Remember to keep your sounds soft, but creative. Try to use different styles of walking with each change.*

Follow Up Ask the group what was funny or interesting about this refocuser.

Showcase If any pair has come up with a particularly interesting walk and sound combination, ask if they would like to demonstrate it to the whole group.

Any
Art
English
History & Geography
Maths
PE
PSHE
Science

Individuals
Partners
Small Group
Whole Group

65 Wrangle Tangle

Any

Art

English

History & Geography

Maths

PE

PSHE

Science

Objective To tangle arms in groups of four or five, then move across the room while tangled.

- Quickly form into small groups.
- *When I give the Start signal, you will stand in a small, tight circle.* Give the signal.
- *The goal here is to get tangled up. Each person, reach in with your right arm and join hands with someone else. You can tangle by going under someone's arm or turning around – anything you like.*
- *Now reach in your other arm and tangle up as much as possible.*
- *Now you are in tangled clumps. As a clump, you must think of a sound you will make together. You have ten seconds to come up with a clump sound.*
- *Now, making your clump sound, your tangled clump must move around*
  the room for 30 seconds. If you meet another clump, figure out how to get around it.
- Signal to start. Allow 30 (or more) seconds. Signal to stop.
- *Untangle – one step at a time – and return to your desks.*

Individuals

Partners

Small Group

Whole Group

Follow Up Discuss the difficulties in moving around as a clump. Are there situations in real life where this might happen (e.g., in crowds in the underground, shopping malls, airports; in mobs)?

66 Explosion!

Objective	To toss and catch an imaginary ball and 'explode' when an unexpected signal is provided.
Props	One small slip of paper per person in an envelope; several slips marked with an X.

- *For this game you will need to stand beside your desks.*
- *I will pass around this envelope. Take a slip, look at it, but keep it secret.*
- *Remember if there is an X on your piece of paper. Now, hide your paper.*
- *Now I am going to call someone's name and throw an imaginary ball to that person. That person must catch the ball, then call another person's name and throw the ball to him or her and so on.*
- *If you had an X on your piece of paper, as soon as you catch the ball, shout 'EXPLODE!' Everyone has to explode loudly and fall to the floor.*
- *You must stay frozen on the floor until I give the 'Get up' signal. Then the person who called 'Explode!' will throw the ball again.*
- *Remember, only certain people can call 'Explode!'. Once a person has called 'Explode!', he or she cannot call it again. So try to remember who has had the ball and who hasn't.*

Any

Art

English

History & Geography

Maths

PE

PSHE

Science

Individuals

Partners

Small Group

Whole Group

67 The Old Duke Revisited

Any

Art

English

History & Geography

Maths

PE

PSHE

Science

Objective To stand and sit in increasingly rapid succession.

- This is a variation on the popular nursery rhyme:

  The Grand Old Duke of York, he had ten thousand men.
  He marched them **up** to the top of the hill and he marched them **down** again.
  And when they were **up,** they were up,
  And when they were **down,** they were down,
  And when they were only **halfway up,** they were neither **up** nor **down.**

- The group must stand up or sit down when each of the words in bold are sung, holding themselves halfway up on the last line, then standing, then sitting.

- Change the words according to the following example:

  Miss Manson's Year X class were restless once again,
  So she marched them **up** to the top of the hill and she marched them **down** again.
  And when they were **up,** they were up,
  And when they were **down,** they were down,
  And when they were only **halfway up,** they were neither **up** nor **down.**

- *This is an action poem.*

- *First I will say a line, then you repeat it.* Recite the entire poem without actions.

- *Now we move up or down on the 'up' or 'down' words. Let's try it slowly.* Practice at least once slowly.

- *Now more quickly!* Continue to increase the speed with each repetition.

Individuals

Partners

Small Group

Whole Group

68 Meet & Greet

Objective To walk around, greeting others in the group in as many unusual ways as possible.

- *When I give you the Start signal, your job will be to move freely around the room, greeting as many people as you can in two minutes.*
- *But there's a catch! You must find unusual ways to greet each other. You can't rely on 'Hi' and a wave. You must be creative.*
- *You might say 'Yo!' or 'Dude!' or even make up a nonsense word for hello.*
- *You might touch fists in greeting or rub shoulders or bow, or wiggle fingers. Be creative.*
- *You can keep changing the way you greet others or stay with one way. You decide.*
- Signal to start, then watch for innovative greetings for showing others later.

Any

Art

English

History & Geography

Maths

PE

PSHE

Science

Individuals

Partners

Small Group

Whole Group

Showcase Ask those who greeted or responded to greetings creatively to demonstrate what they did.

69 Mad Milling

Any

Art

English

History & Geography

Maths

PE

PSHE

Science

Objective To move around the room in the different styles or in the persona of different characters. You could select characters from books the group are reading.

- *When I give the Start signal, move to …* Indicate an open area of the room or suggest moving carefully around furniture.
- *You will be milling about. That means walking around, not touching anyone or interfering with their space.*
- *But the fun is that you will be listening to my suggestions and walking according to them.*
- *You can also make any sounds that might accompany specific movements.*
- *For example, if I say 'Walk on hot coals', you might lift your feet quickly and say, 'Ouch! Ouch!'*
- *When you hear the signal again, freeze and wait for the next instruction.*

Extended Follow Up Challenge the group to choose one form of movement and expand on it in writing; e.g., a story about someone who moves that way.

Showcase Invite the group to demonstrate various movements.

Individuals

Partners

Small Group

Whole Group

Suggested Movements

Walking on
- Ice
- Broken glass
- Eggs
- Soft fur

Walking as a
- Very old person
- Puppet
- Toy soldier
- Injured warrior
- Ninja

Walking through/in
- Deep water
- Mud
- Tall grasses
- Snakes

Walking while feeling
- Tired
- Extremely happy
- Cold
- Afraid
- Sick

70 Kodak Moments

Objective To spontaneously create and hold perfect poses.

- *You've might have heard the term 'Kodak moment'. It means a picture-perfect moment, a time when people are perfectly posed to have their photo taken.*
- *You and your partner/group will have 60 seconds to create and hold a perfect Kodak moment.*
- *But here's where the fun comes in. I will tell you who you will be portraying before you arrange the pose.*
- *You can discuss the Kodak moment with your partners, but you need to move very quickly. I'll tell you when the first 30 seconds is up.*
- *Let's see who can come up with the most creative poses.*
- *You will be working beside your desks (in the space at the back of the room, etc.). Remember not to move into the space of another pair (group).*
- *Once you have your pose, hold it – freeze it.*
- Begin the signal.

Extended Follow Up Challenge the group to write (a story, a news article, a diary entry, etc.) about the people portrayed in the picture.

Showcase Invite the groups to look around at the poses of others before unfreezing everyone and/or moving to a new moment.

Suggestions for 'Kodak Moments'

- Family of teddy bears
- Group of superheroes
- Millionaire family
- Family of supermodels
- Family of hillbillies (or any geographically based group)
- Group of ballet dancers (or other kind of dancers)
- Group of nursery school children
- Group of angry mobsters
- Group of nuns and priests
- Members of a sports team

Any

Art

English

History & Geography

Maths

PE

PSHE

Science

Individuals

Partners

Small Group

Whole Group

4 Let's Communicate

Single Words & Sounds

The motivators in this section require cooperation; in many cases group members will be fast-talking in some manner with neighbours or nearby small groups. At other times, they will be making appropriate sounds to accompany actions. For the most part, these motivators involve individuals conversing or communicating within the protective confines of the entire group. They are completely independent, but still collective, activities that culminate in magical minutes of sound making. These motivators involve considerable cognition and creativity, as well as short-term memory. In addition, they encourage social constructivism or learning from peers, making them excellent for diverse groups where some members may be less fluent with the language or less capable communicators, thus benefitting from interaction.

- In these activities, basic literacy skills come into play in an entertaining, motivating and almost magical manner – plus talking is allowed and encouraged within the limitations of the activity.
- Many of these 3-Minute Motivators benefit from Follow Ups.
- Many of the activities in this section lead well into further individual tasks, such as writing or researching.

These motivators work well at times when the class is fidgety but not focusing, when they are restless and not directing their thoughts to the lesson at hand: for example, following a video, story-reading or Art class; and before a more focused literacy task, such as writing or cognitive class, such as Maths.

71 Talk-a-Lot

Any

Art

English

History & Geography

Maths

PE

PSHE

Science

Objective To talk non-stop about anything for a full 60 seconds.

- This activity works best when groups have been excessively chatty, as it beats them at their own game.
- *It seems you all need some talking time. Okay, you have exactly one minute to talk.*
- *You must talk for a whole minute, but when I give the Stop signal, you must stop immediately and face me.*
- *Remember – everyone must talk when I say, 'Go'. Everyone will be talking at the same time. Get all you have to say out in one minute. You'll be surprised how long a minute can be.*
- *GO!*
- I have never had groups continue talking after the Stop signal. They are so amazed that you have asked them to talk that they readily adhere to the limits.

Individuals (as part of Whole Group)

Partners

Small Group

Whole Group

72 Interactive Words

Objective To chant words as they are broken into pieces.

- Write a fairly lengthy word on the board.
- Prompt the group: *Say after me.*
- This is a chanting activity. Begin saying the word repeatedly, each time dropping a single letter from the beginning:
  - *SPAGHETTI*
  - *PAGHETTI*
  - *AGHETTI*
  - *GHETTI*
  - *HETTI*
  - *ETTI*
  - *TTI*
  - *TI*
  - *I*
- After you have demonstrated, write other words and invite different group members to lead the chant.
- Choosing words from core curriculum (e.g., equilateral, dinosaur) is a way to reinforce vocabulary, spelling, phonetic awareness and fun!

Any
Art
English
History & Geography
Maths
PE
PSHE
Science

Individuals
Partners
Small Group
Whole Group

73 Oscar

Any

Art

English (phonetic awareness)

History & Geography

Maths

PE

PSHE

Science

Objective To say 'Oscar' every time a certain word or sound is heard.

Props A short piece to read aloud.

- *Sit comfortably in your desks, feet on the floor, facing me. Don't slouch, because you will need to be very alert!*
- *I am going to read from …* (name the text).
- *Every time you hear the 's' sound at the beginning of a word (or* -ing *ending; words that rhymes with …), you must shout out 'Oscar!'*
- The reading selection can be a picture book, a piece of poetry, a section from a textbook or novel - whatever you wish.
- This activity is a favourite with all ages. The word 'Oscar' is an amusing and easy-to-say word that children enjoy shouting; however, any word can be used.
- If a word from a specific subject (e.g., 'isosceles', 'equilateral', 'ecosystem', 'revolution') needs reinforcing, use that instead of 'Oscar'. To increase the difficulty, simply alter what the group must listen for: e.g., *Listen for any words related to ecosystems and shout 'Ecosystem!' when you hear one.*

Individuals (as part of Whole Group)

Partners

Small Group

Whole Group

74 Count-Off

Objective To attempt to count as high as possible, one person at a time.

- *Sit comfortably in your desks, feet on the floor, eyes front.*
- *You are going to count as high as possible as a group. Sounds easy doesn't it? How high do you think we can count?* Ask for suggestions.
- *But here's the tricky part. Anyone can say a number, but if two or more people say the number at the same time, we have to start all over again.*
- *You can turn around so that you can see everyone, but stay in your seats. Watch and listen carefully so that no two people speak at the same time.*
- *No more than three seconds can go by between numbers.*
- *Start counting.*
- This is quite challenging. It's difficult to say a number without someone else saying it too. Most groups never get past 5 or 6.

75 Hip-Hip-Hooray

Any

Art

English (phonetic awareness)

History & Geography

Maths

PE

PSHE

Science

Objective To combine word parts into wholes and chant three times quickly, like a cheer.

- *This is a game where we all get to shout 'Hip-hip-hooray!', and throw our arms in the air. Let's try it!*
- *Now wave your arms three times as if we were shouting 'Hip Hip Hooray!' or giving three cheers, such as 'Rah! Rah! Rah!'.* Demonstrate if necessary.
- *I am going to give you a long word, but I will say it stretched out, sound by sound.*
- *Like this: ca-ter-pil-lar.*
- *You will put the sounds together like three cheers. When you've finished, shout 'Hip-hip-hooray!' and throw your arms up!*
- 'Ca-ter-pil-lar' will sound like 'CATERPILLAR! CATERPILLAR! CATERPILLAR! HIP-HIP-HOORAY!'

Extended Follow Up If used with older groups, ask them to write down a couple of their favourite words and, when the interrupted session is complete, discuss what the words mean and use them in sentences.

Although this is a sound-blending game suitable for young children, it works surprisingly well with older students too, especially if lengthy, interesting words area used. The following suggestions are divided by difficulty.

Easier		**More Difficult**	
Multiply	Kindergarten	Personification	Serendipity
Family	Paper	Appaloosa	Misdemeanour
Communicate	Happy	Conundrum	Derogatory
Alphabet	City	Cybernetics	Vestibule
Banana	Summer	Monologue	Trajectory
Dinosaur	Winter	Periodical	Precipitate
Woman	Butterfly	Onomatopoeia	Rigmarole
		Objectionable	Personification

Individuals (as part of Whole Group)

Partners

Small Group

Whole Group

76 Chant-Along

Objective To chant simple words/text with others

Props Short verses suitable for chanting

- *Sit straight in your desks, feet on the floor, eyes on me.*
- *Don't lean against the chair backs. Sit tall.*
- *We are going to chant together.*
- If groups can read, put the chants on overheads or the board. Otherwise, use the 'I say, you say' method and repeat the chant several times until the group have memorised it.

Any

Art

English

History & Geography

Maths

PE

PSHE

Science

Follow Up Discuss with the group why chanting has a calming effect.

Individuals (as part of Whole Group)

Partners

Small Group

Whole Group

Suggested Chants

1 Slowly I go, slowly I know, and slowly I grow – Slow! Slow! Slow!
2 I close my eyes, I close my ears. I say good-bye to hurts and fears.
3 The hurry in my head I cease, I fill it up with gentle peace. I close my eyes and beauty see. I deeply breathe, and calm I'll be.
4 One and two and three and four, I'm counting now, peace to restore. Five and six and seven too – relaxing, calming through and through.
5 Pitter patter falls the rain, making all seem clean again. Gently, softly falling down, in sparkling puddles all around.

77 Animal Farm

Any

Art

English

History & Geography

Maths

PE

PSHE

Science

Objective To participate, using animal sounds, in a whole-group animal chorus.

- *We are going to become an animal chorus.*
- Break the class into five or six equal parts (i.e., tables or rows), and assign each group one of the following animals: cows, chickens, ducks, horses, donkeys, pigs, dogs, cats.
- *First we need to practice the sounds these animals make.* Ask each group, in unison, make the appropriate sounds.
- *You all know the tune to …* Choose something familiar, such as 'Three Blind Mice', 'Twinkle, Twinkle Little Star' or 'Jingle Bells'.
- *Now we will make our animal sounds to the tune, starting with one group at a time, and then all together.*
- Begin by getting each group to sing a line of the tune using the animal sounds; then get the entire group to sing together.

Individuals (as part of Whole Group)

Partners

Small Group

Whole Group

78 Punctuate This!

Objective To become punctuation marks for a piece of text or reading.

Props An display of sentences with punctuation missing (optional).

- On the board, write a sentence containing a variety of punctuation:
- e.g., The boy, his face red, shouted, 'Where's my ball?'
- *We are going to* ***be*** *the punctuation for this sentence. Let's think of sounds or actions that will represent each of the punctuation marks.*
- Allow the group to be creative. Actions can accompany sounds.
- *Now, each time we need one of these punctuation marks, you will make the sound, do the action.*
- After a practice run, give the class sentences, at an appropriate level. Encourage verbal and physical interaction with the punctuation marks.
- e.g., The boy (*squeak*) his face red (*squeak*) shouted (*squeak*) shouted (*squeak; click, click*) Where (*mmmmmm*) s my ball (*wooooo; click, click*).

Any

Art

English

History & Geography

Maths

PE

PSHE

Science

Individuals (as part of Whole Group)

Partners

Small Group

Whole Group

Suggested Actions
- Full stop = clap once • Exclamation mark = 'Bang!'
- Comma = 'Squeak' • Colon = 'Beep! Beep!'
- Question mark = 'Woooooo' • Semi-colon = 'Beep, Ahhhhh'
- Quotation marks = two clicks • Apostrophe = 'Mmmmmmm'

79 Alphabet Pyramid

Any

Art

English

History & Geography

Maths

PE

PSHE

Science

Objective To think of words starting with consecutive letters of the alphabet.

- *Sit in your chair facing your partner/the group.*
- *You will take turns speaking.*
- *I will give you a subject to talk about, but every word you say must begin with the next letter of the alphabet in sequence.*
- *For example, I might start with 'apple', then the next person would say 'banana', then I could say 'cake', and so on.*
- *Here's the catch – your words must build a pyramid, so must be repeated once more than the previous word.*
- *So it would go 'apple', 'banana, banana', 'cake, cake, cake', then maybe 'donut, donut, donut, donut' and so on.*
- *All the words you say must fit the theme I give you. What theme was I using for the words I have just used?*

Individuals

Partners

Small Group

Whole Group

Suggested Themes

- School
- Summer holidays
- My favourite things
- Brothers or sisters
- Homework
- The forest/mountains/ocean/lake/river

80 Popcorn

Objective To make tiny bouncing movements and popping sounds, like popcorn popping.

- *Sit tall in your seat and keep your feet on the floor at all times during this activity.*
- *You are going to be pieces of popcorn in a popper.*
- *When I give the Start signal, start popping: bounce up a little on your chairs and make a small 'pop' sound each time you bounce.*
- *We will bounce slowly at first – just like when popcorn starts off.*
- *Then we'll gradually get faster and louder as I signal you.*
- *As you pop, try to go from tiny piece of corn to puffy popcorn.*
- Keep coaching to increase speed and loudness.

Any
Art
English
History & Geography
Maths
PE
PSHE
Science

Individuals (as part of Whole Group)
Partners
Small Group
Whole Group

81 Clap 3

Any

Art

English

History & Geography

Maths

PE

PSHE

Science

Objective To maintain a verbal sequence of numbers or counting, but to substitute a clap for every 3 or multiple of 3.

- *This is a counting game. We will start at one side of the room and just keep counting the numbers in sequence.*
- *But here's the challenge! You mustn't say the number 3 or any multiple of 3. Instead you must clap.*
- *For example, it would go like this: one, two,* clap, *four, five,* clap, *seven, eight,* clap *– and so on.*
- *Now here's where it gets really exciting. If a number even has a 3 in it, you must clap for the 3:*
- *For example, for 31 you must do this:* Clap, *one*
- *There are no winners or losers here. We are working together to see how high and fast we can count.*
- This can be simplified for younger groups by using more simple rules: e.g., every other person claps; every number with a 2 in it claps.

Individuals

Partners

Small Group

Whole Group

82 The Numbered Letter

Objective To quickly think of a word starting with a specific letter.

- *For this game I will start you off with a word and a number. You and your partner must say words that begin with the letter that comes in the numbered position in the word.*
- *For example, if I say 'school' and '3', you and your partner must say words that begin with the third letter in 'school' – the letter 'h'.*
- *The trick is to go as fast as you can.*
- *No repeating, no mumbling or hesitations.*
- *If your partner makes a mistake, then you win the first round. Just start again and keep going until I tell you to stop.*
- Difficulty can be increased by choosing a theme for the words; e.g., all words must be related to a part of the curriculum. This works well as vocabulary reinforcement for a specific subject.

83 If You're Happy …

Any

Art

English

History & Geography

Maths

PE

PSHE

Science

Objective To participate in group exploration of the familiar tune 'If You're Happy and You Know It'.

- Familiarise group with the song:

  If you're happy and you know it clap your hands (*clap clap*)
  If you're happy and you know it clap your hands (*clap clap*)
  If you're happy and you know it and you really want to show it.
  If you're happy and you know it clap your hands (*clap clap*)

- *First we have to think of something else we might feel or do, instead of feeling happiness.* Invite ideas and suggestions for actions to go with them instead of clapping.
- *Now we'll sing the song with our new ideas and add the actions.*
- *Once we've added a couple of verses, we'll begin at the beginning with 'happy' and put them all together.*
- Success of this motivator depends on quickly establishing a couple of other emotions or activities and associated actions.

Individuals (as part of Whole Group)

Partners

Small Group

Whole Group

Suggested Actions

- Angry: stamp your feet
- Tired: stretch your arms
- Lonely: hug yourself
- Itchy: shake your legs
- Restless: shake your hands
- Leaving: wave good-bye
- Frightened: bite your nails
- Hungry: rub your tummy

84 Quick Catch

Objective To throw and catch an imaginary object.

- *For this game we will need to pay close attention to each other, because we are going to be throwing and catching an imaginary object.*
- *You can decide what the object is: small ball, a football, a sword, a marble, a paper aeroplane, a heavy steel ball, a bowling ball, a pencil – whatever you can think of.*
- *First you will need to catch whatever has been thrown to you.*
- *Then you must call the name of the person you are throwing to and quickly say what you are throwing.*
- *The fun of the game is that we must work cooperatively. That means we have to try to remember who has already been thrown to and throw to someone else until everyone has had a turn.*
- *Think of what you might throw. Of course you can always throw a ball.*
- *I'll start. I am throwing an egg to …* (group member). *He will have to catch it carefully, so as not to break it. When he has it he will say, 'Got it!' Then he'll call a name and throw something different.*

Any

Art

English

History & Geography

Maths

PE

PSHE

Science

Individuals (as part of Whole Group)

Partners

Small Group

Whole Group

Follow Up Quickly discuss what was easy or difficult to catch.

Conversation

For the 3-Minute Motivators in this section, group members work together, communicating by quickly responding to cues in order to carry on conversations in an unusual or controlled manner. In some cases, the conversations lead to a further activity, such as following a verbal direction with an action. In all cases, the dialogues involve quick thinking, careful listening, organisational skills and communication skills.

These motivators lend themselves to situations where groups need to focus on communication of all kinds – media, text, visual – as well as culturally divergent forms of communication, dialects and languages. The tasks ask the group to experiment with many varieties of communicative techniques in rapid, fun-filled, concentrated ways.

- These motivators make excellent starting points for all manner of follow-up writing and discussing. In fact, many of them will leave the group with new insights into common everyday situations, as well as a variety of ideas for problem solving. These thoughts can become extended lessons.
- Since all these activities involve working with a partner, it may be a good idea to find ways to introduce variety in partners. Rather than always having people pair with the 'the person next to you', try 'every second person' or 'person on the opposite side of the table or row'. Just keep in mind that any movement to get to a partner can interfere with the three-minute time limit.

Conversation activities may well be the most popular 3-Minute Motivators. Groups love them; leaders appreciate their refocusing qualities, as well as the inherent learning they provide. In most cases, some form of discourse ensues – often entertaining, even hilarious, dialogue.

85 Song Speak

Any

Art

English

History & Geography

Maths

PE

PSHE

Science

Objective To communicate only in song or melody.

- *Sit at your desks, facing your partner, feet on the floor and hands in your laps.*
- *The two of you are going to carry on a conversation entirely in song. You can choose any subject you want, but you have to sing it.*
- *I will give you a topic to talk about.*
- *Remember to take turns 'song speaking'.*
- Demonstrate in song. Use a simple tune like 'Three Blind Mice' if you don't feel creative.

All of you,
Yes, all of you,
Will talk in song,
In lovely, lovely song,
About what you did last Saturday,
Or maybe even Sunday.
Sing/speak about your weekend.
Start singing now!

Individuals

Partners

Small Group

Whole Group

86 I Am You

Objective To carry on a conversation 'in the shoes of' a partner.

- If small groups can be readily formed use them; otherwise, stick to partners for the sake of expediency.
- *You and you partners are going to carry out a discussion, but you must talk as if you actually **are** your partner.* Demonstrate by choosing two group members:
- *I am Mark* (Sue is speaking). *I like playing rugby. I am good at it.*
- *I am Sue* (Mark is speaking). *I am good at school work.*
- (Sue speaking) *Someday I will be a famous rugby star.*
- *I will give you something to talk about. You will discuss what you like and dislike. Maybe even what your pet hates are, but no put downs – only positive comments. And remember you ARE the other person.*

Any

Art

English

History & Geography

Maths

PE

PSHE

Science

Individuals

Partners

Small Group

Whole Group

Extended Follow Up This is a great activity to talk about at length at a later time. Discuss what it felt like having another person talking about you to your face, saying good things about you, being you. Follow up with writing about anything learned about self.

87 Alphabet Game

Any (as source of themes)

Art

English

History & Geography

Maths

PE

PSHE

Science

Objective To carry on a conversation in which each sentence begins with the next letter of the alphabet.

- *You need to remember your alphabet for this game.* Refer the class to individual alphabet sheets or an alphabet on the wall.
- *I am going to tell you what to talk about, then you and your partner/group will discuss the topic. Each person must say a complete sentence. The **first** word of each sentence will begin with whatever letter comes next in the alphabet. For example, on the theme of Homework*:
- **A** lot of kids hate homework
- **B**ut I am not one of those kids.
- **C**an you tell me why?
- **D**on't know!
- **E**very time I get homework, I hate it.
- *If someone can't think of a sentence in a few seconds, that person is out. You could end up with a winner or you could both get all the way through the alphabet.*
- The competitive aspect of this activity can be omitted and the game can be entirely cooperative. For younger children, just saying words according to a theme or making the conversation themeless, can simplify the game.

Individuals

Partners

Small Group

Whole Group

Follow Up It can be a lot of fun if two group members want to face-off before the entire group and attempt the game for all to hear and enjoy. A good choice of themes helps to keep the situation amusing.

88 Slow-Mo

Objective To carry on a discussion that continually switches from fast speaking to slow motion.

- *This is a talking game.*
- *You and your partner will talk about a topic that I will provide.*
- *The catch is that you must talk either very quickly – as if someone has put you on fast forward – or very slowly in s-l-o-w m-o-t-i-o-n.*
- *You will change from one to the other every time you hear my signal.*
- *It doesn't matter who is talking when you hear the signal. Just continue the conversation, but change the speed.*
- *Remember – in any good conversation, both people get a chance to speak.*
- Signal to start.
- Signal to change speeds every few seconds.

Any
Art
English
History & Geography
Maths
PE
PSHE
Science

Individuals
Partners
Small Group
Whole Group

Showcase Invite group members to share a short dialogue, just for the entertainment value.

89 A Quantity of Questions

Any

Art

English

History & Geography

Maths

PE

PSHE

Science

Objective To carry on a conversation, based on a specific theme, using questions alone.

- *Turn to face your partner.*
- *You are going to carry on a conversation about …* Provide a theme.
- *But the catch is you must only speak using questions. For example, if I was talking to my partner about school, the conversation might go like this:*

  Do you like school?
  Do you?
  I think you do, don't you?
  Do you think our teacher is good?
  Are you asking me if I like our teacher?

- *Remember to use* ***only*** *questions. If one of you forgets to use a question, you are both out. Let's see how long you and your partner can last. You will need to help each other.*

Individuals

Partners

Small Group

Whole Group

Follow Up Ask the group to talk about what they found difficult about this activity. If you want to develop the experience further, invite two volunteers to play off against each other for the entertainment of the group.

Suggested Themes

- Video games
- Sports
- Food
- Clothing and fashion
- TV
- Homework
- Brothers and sisters
- Parents
- Pets

90 You Did What?

Objective To quickly and spontaneously create in a small group three or four sentences about a nonsensical topic.

- Quickly divide into groups of four or five, sitting in small circles either at tables or on the floor.
- *I will give you a silly topic, called a 'lead statement'.*
- *Every lead statement will begin with 'What did you do when …'*
- *We will move around the circle and each person will say the first thing that comes into their head about the topic.*
- *For example, if the lead statement is, 'What did you do when you woke up in the middle of the jungle?' I might say, 'First, I started to scream. But when I saw some monkeys swinging through the trees, I decided to join them'.*
- *Decide who will speak first in each group; I want that person to put up his or her hand to show me.*
- *I might use my Stop signal to change the topic before it gets all the way around the circle, so listen out for that.*
- *If anyone wants to use the Pass on one turn, that's okay. But no more than one Pass per person.*

Any | Art | **English** | History & Geography | Maths | PE | PSHE | Science

Individuals | Partners | **Small Group** | Whole Group

Suggested Lead Statements

What did you do when …

… your pet started talking to you?
… you landed on the moon in your newly built space shuttle?
… you opened your cupboard to find Homer Simpson (or Brad Pitt, Elvis Presley)?
… you looked in the mirror and had no reflection?
… you ate a sweet and suddenly found yourself shrinking?
… you suddenly had the ability to fly (or other superhero power)?

91 You DON'T Say!

Any

Art

English

History & Geography

Maths

PE

PSHE

Science

Objective To carry on a conversation without ever using certain words.

- *This game is a talking game where you must carry on a conversation with your partner, but you cannot use certain words.*
- *For example, you can't use 'and' or 'I' in this conversation.*
- *If someone uses 'and' or 'I', that person is out and the other one is the winner.*
- *For example, if I wanted to say 'Last night I stayed at home and did my homework', I'd have to say, 'Last night this person stayed at home. This person did their homework'.*
- *If one of you is out, you can start again if there's time left.*
- *I will tell you what to talk about and which words you must not use.*
- *Begin when I give the Start signal.*

Individuals

Partners

Small Group

Whole Group

Follow Up Quickly discuss how difficult it is to exclude particular words from dialogue. Are some more difficult than others?

Suggested Words to Eliminate

• The • My • But • And • I

Suggested Topics

- What you do every morning to get ready for school.
- How you feel about … (friends, boy/girl friends, parents, brothers and sisters, homework, school, teachers, bedtimes)

92 'Yes, But' Pet Peeves

Objective To carry on an escalating conversation about pet peeves, in which each speaker has a worse peeve than the previous one.

- *Sit facing your partner.*
- *I will give you a topic to talk about and provide the opening sentence. Then you will begin to speak one at a time. You are to carry on a to-and-fro conversation for a full two minutes.*
- *You must each start what you say with, 'Yes, but ...' and find something wrong with what the last person said.*
- *For example, if the starter is 'The stars are pretty', the first person might say, 'Yes, but they are far away'. Then the next person might say, 'Yes, but you can see them with your telescope and I can't', and so on.*
- Provide a theme and give the start signal.

Any

Art

English

History & Geography

Maths

PE

PSHE

Science

Extended Follow Up *When do we use 'Yes, but ... ' in day-to-day conversation? When we use 'Yes, but ... ' what are we saying or doing to what the other person said?*

Possible Starters

- School is really tough
- My dog ran away
- I forgot my lunch today
- My mum has to go to work
- It's raining and we can't have ...
- I spent all my allowance on sweets
- My friend's dad bought a new car

Individuals

Partners

Small Group

Whole Group

93 Glad Game

Any

Art

English

History & Geography

Maths

PE

PSHE

Science

Objective To carry on a conversation in which partners complete the sentence beginning 'I am glad … '

- *Sit facing your partner.*
- *You are to carry on a to-and-fro conversation for a full two minutes.*
- *You must each start what you say with 'I am glad … '*
- *For example, I might say, 'I am glad I am here today', and my partner might say, 'I am glad I have done my homework'.*
- *What one person says doesn't have to relate to what their partner has said; you simply have to keep thinking of what you are glad about.*
- *You must keep talking until I stop you.*

Individuals

Partners

Small Group

Whole Group

Extended Follow Up *Recall as many things as possible that you said you were glad about and write them down. Choose one to write about in more detail.*

94 Just a Minute

Objective To keep talking on a subject for a full 60 seconds, without stopping or mumbling.

- *Face your partner and decide who is A and who is B.*
- *When I give the Start signal, Partner A must begin talking – the catch is that I will tell A what to talk about. A must keep talking about that subject until I say 'Stop'.*
- *Then it will be Partner B's turn, but with a different subject.*
- *You will each talk for a full 60 seconds, without repeating yourself, saying 'ah' or 'erm', tripping over your tongue or taking more than two seconds to think. It's harder than it seems.*
- *Now, before we start, put up your hand if you think you'll be able to do this.*
- *If you put up your hand, draw a tiny star on your page. Your partner will decide at the end whether you deserve your star or not.*
- *If you didn't give yourself a star, your partner might decide after your turn that you deserve one.*
- *Let's see how well we know ourselves and our communication abilities.*
- Any curriculum-related topic works well with older students and serves to reinforce learning.

Any
Art
English
History & Geography
Maths
PE
PSHE
Science

Follow Up Find out who earned a star. Discuss the reasons why some people did and others didn't.

Suggested General Topics
- Favourite foods
- When I grow up
- Caring for a pet
- Parents and siblings
- Summer holidays

Suggested Subject-related Topics
- Writing an essay
- Doing a science experiment
- Solving a maths problem
- Life in an ecosystem
- Making an electrical circuit
- Creating an object from clay

Individuals
Partners
Small Group
Whole Group

95 Fortunately/Unfortunately

Any

Art

English

History & Geography

Maths

PE

PSHE

Science

Objective To converse with a partner where one person always begins their sentences with 'Fortunately', while the other begins with 'Unfortunately'.

- *Sit facing your partner.*
- *Decide who is A and who is B.*
- *You are to carry on a to-and-fro conversation for a full two minutes.*
- *You must start what you say with 'Fortunately' or 'Unfortunately'.*
- *Partner B will start. B will be 'Fortunately'. Partner A will be 'Unfortunately'.*
- *For example, B might say, 'Fortunately today is Friday'. Then A could respond, 'Unfortunately, we have been given homework for the weekend'.*
- *When I signal to swap, you will start your sentences with the opposite word.*
- Signal to start. Continue for about one minute, then switch roles.

Individuals

Partners

Small Group

Whole Group

Follow Up What did the group learn? There can always be a 'fortunate' or an 'unfortunate' depending on our outlook.

Extended Follow Up Ask the group to create comparison charts for which they think of opposing 'fortunates' for any 'unfortunates' they may have.

96 I Appreciate …

Objective To brainstorm, alternating with a partner, as many appreciated people, things, or ideas as possible.

- *Sit comfortably facing your partner/neighbour/friend.*
- *When I give the Start signal, you will take turns saying 'I appreciate … ' and completing the sentence.*
- Demonstrate: *I appreciate everyone in my group. I appreciate the fact that my car started today. I appreciate the good lunch I packed for myself.*
- Point out that the group's appreciation can be for abstract concepts as well as actual people, places or things.
- Signal to start.
- Let the communication continue for up to two minutes, then signal to stop.
- *Now I want each of you to recall one thing your partner appreciated. Tell your partner why your liked that particular appreciation.*

Any
Art
English
History & Geography
Maths
PE
PSHE
Science

Individuals
Partners
Small Group
Whole Group

Follow Up Ask the group if they learned anything by participating in this activity. Do the group realise that we all have lots to appreciate.

97 May There Be ...

Any

Art

English

History & Geography

Maths

PE

PSHE

Science

Objective To discuss possibilities.

- *This is a game of imagining and wishing.*
- *All you have to do is take turns completing the sentence starters 'May there be ... ' or 'May there never be ... '*
- *Decide who is A and who is B.*
- *Partner B, you will start with 'May there be ... '*
- *Partner A, you will say 'May there never be ... '*
- *You will continue this for three sentences each – six sentences altogether. Then you'll swap and A will start with 'May there be ... '*
- *What kinds of things might you say? How about 'May there be sunshine today'. 'May there never be a hurricane here'.*
- *It doesn't matter what you say – just let your imaginations go.*
- *At the end of the time, we'll try to remember some of the ideas.*
- Signal to start.
- Stop after a couple of minutes or if the group gets bogged down.

Individuals

Partners

Small Group

Whole Group

Extended Follow Up Explore the possibility of writing poems based on the ideas that have been generated.

98 Third-Person Talk

Objective To carry on a discussion in the third person.

- *This is a curious game of communication.*
- *You will have a discussion with your partner about something you will do or have done, BUT you have to speak about yourself in third person.*
- *In other words, instead of saying 'I did . . . ' I would will need to say 'David did . . . ' Instead of saying 'give it to me', I would say 'give it to* David.
- *This is harder than it sounds.*
- *I will give you a topic to discuss.*
- *When I give the Start signal, you must talk for two full minutes in third person.*

Any

Art

English

History & Geography

Maths

PE

PSHE

Science

Follow Up Briefly discuss what was difficult and when such a manner of speech might be used.

Extended Follow Up Challenge the group to write a story in third person.

Showcase Invite any pair who have done well to put on a brief discussion for the class.

Suggested Topics

- What I did last weekend (or on holiday)
- When I grow up . . .
- My life with . . . (specific family members)
- When I was younger . . .
- My first experience with a dentist (or a doctor, hospital, health nurse)

Individuals

Partners

Small Group

Whole Group

99 Hi-Lo Speak

Any

Art

English

History & Geography

Maths

PE

PSHE

Science

Objective To be physically higher or lower than a partner when speaking.

- *In this game, the person who is talking must always be higher than the listener.*
- *For example, if I am talking with Ruth, when I talk, I must be standing and raise myself up to be much higher than Ruth.*
- *But when she speaks, even if it's just to say 'Yes' or 'No', she must be higher than I am.*
- *The idea is that the speaker is always looking down at the listener.*
- *To make it really fun, each person should not talk for long. The shorter your sentence or reply, the more quickly the two of you will have to adjust your positions.*
- *Think of what would happen in a 'Yes – No – Yes – No' argument.*
- *When I give the signal, you will begin talking about the subject I will provide and continue until I signal you to stop.*
- For suggested topics, see 'Third-Person Talk' on page 125.

Individuals

Partners

Small Group

Whole Group

Follow Up Quickly discuss what was fun or difficult about this.

Extended Follow Up With older groups, this lends itself to more in-depth discussions about being higher or lower than others metaphorically.

Note *Since groups will work together to come up with quantities of brainstormed words, ideas or thoughts, they usually require paper and pencils to record their ideas. Younger groups can, of course, draw their ideas rather than writing them down or ideas can be called out and written down by the group leader.*

Brainstorm

The 3-Minute Motivators in this section are designed for pair or even team work; they are socially constructive in nature and cover many strands of the English curriculum. Groups will work together to quickly brainstorm ideas based on suggestions from the group leader. They might be jotting these ideas on paper, reading them and sharing them, all in rapid succession. In fact, because these motivators are carried out under time pressure and because they are generally competitive in nature, they become quite heart-thumping experiences.

These activities engage groups in imaginative thought, quick thinking and rapid recall of information. They are both cognitive and stimulating in nature. Consequently these motivators are great for revving up sleepy brains, for jump-starting lethargic imaginations and for generally engrossing groups in an exciting and challenging manner, so that they return to an interrupted topic with renewed vigour. Some of these refocusers may seem similar to those in the Conversation section; the difference lies in the fact that most of these motivators require only single-word responses and are done more quickly and spontaneously. Even those requiring more of a sentence or phrase response are of a brainstorming or listing nature.

- Follow Up and Extended Follow Up can be valuable for the activities in this section, as many of them can be expanded into worthwhile writing, research or discussion topics.
- Since many of these activities are timed challenges between partners, prizes definitely enhance the fun element. The mere idea of a prize can elevate participants' level of commitment.

100 2-for-10 Tales

Any

Art

English

History & Geography

Maths

PE

PSHE

Science

Objective To cooperate to create a ten-sentence story, complete with protagonist, plot, climax etc.

- *Sit facing your partner.*
- *Together you are going to create (write, tell) a story about …* Provide theme.
- *But here's the catch. You must use exactly ten sentences!*
- *There are two of you, so that means you have to take turns and each provide five sentences to make up your story.*
- *And it must make sense. Think of all the things that make a good story – characters, plot, beginning, ending – and be sure to get them all into exactly ten sentences.*
- *You will have two minutes to complete your story, so you'll have to work quickly.*
- Signal to start.
- After two minutes (or more time if desired), signal to stop.

Individuals

Partners

Small Group

Whole Group

Follow Up *What was hard about this task?*

Extended Follow Up Ask the group to write their stories out for display, sticking to the ten-sentence rule and participate in a whole-group discussion at a later time.

Showcase Invite a couple of pairs to share their stories. Carefully check for exact number of sentences.

Point Please?

Objective To look at a familiar situation from different points of view.

Props Point-of-View cards (optional)

- *For this game you will need to think in unusual way, but also think quickly and brainstorm together.*
- *I will give you a situation that is familiar to all of us; for example, 'a rainy day'.*
- *Your job is to think of and write down as many different ways as possible to look at or think of a rainy day. For example:*
- *A disappointment for people going on a picnic*
- *Great for farmers in a drought*
- *Good for fish or ducks*
- *Bad news for people living near a high river*
- *This will be a competition. The pair/group with the most 'good' points of view will win.*
- Signal to start.
- Don't allow more than about two minutes. Keep it snappy.
- Signal to stop.

Any
Art
English
History & Geography
Maths
PE
PSHE
Science

Follow Up Count up to find a winner, then discuss these view points with the group.

Extended Follow Up Take the idea of different view points into literature or other subjects (e.g., Geography: point of view of displaced persons) and discuss. Or challenge the group to write from an unfamiliar point of view.

You could make cards containing point-of-view starters, so they can be reused, e.g.:

- Being a victim of a natural disaster: forest fire, flood, earthquake, storm
- Losing something of value: wallet, ID, pet, sentimental jewellery
- The person in a story who steals from someone
- A very hot day in the desert

Individuals
Partners
Small Group
Whole Group

102 And the Real Meaning Is …

Any

Art

English

History & Geography

Maths

PE

PSHE

Science

Individuals

Partners

Small Group

Whole Group

Objective To brainstorm as many original and humorous meanings of common words as possible.

Note This game may be too difficult for children younger than about the age of eight.

- *For this game I am going to give you a common word; you and your partner are to brainstorm as many different ways to describe the meaning of the word as you can. For example, if the word was 'lazy', you might say:*
- *People who leave their clothes on all night so they don't have to get dressed in the morning.*
- *A person who lies on top of the bed so he doesn't have to make the bed.*
- *Someone who eats soup out of the tin so she doesn't have to wash a saucepan.*
- *You will need to be really creative, maybe even silly.*
- *Remember, you aren't actually giving the definition of the word. You are explaining what the word means when it is being used to describe someone or something.*
- *I will give you two minutes to brainstorm ideas and jot them down.*
- *Then we will discuss some of the ideas.*

Extended Follow Up Use the brainstormed ideas as writing projects, working them into a story or character description.

Suggested Words

- Happy
- Famous
- Compulsive
- Goodhearted
- Workaholic
- Bored
- Evil
- Silly
- Tired
- Infamous
- Predictable

103 Synonym Sense

Objective To quickly brainstorm synonyms for common words.

Props Pencil & paper

- Pair the group.
- *I am going to provide a word and you are to work together to think of as many other words as you can that mean the same or almost the same, thing. You will jot down all the words you come up with.*
- *You will have 20 seconds per word.*
- *This is a competition: after two minutes (that is, four words), we will compare your lists to find the winning pair!*
- It's a good idea to do a quick one together to demonstrate:
- *For the word 'Say': speak, utter, talk, chat, verbalise, lecture, address, tell, cry, announce, exclaim, reply, shout.*
- Give the first word. After 20 seconds, give the second word and so on for four words.
- Signal to stop.

Any
Art
English
History & Geography
Maths
PE
PSHE
Science

Individuals
Partners
Small Group
Whole Group

Words with Many Synonyms
• Look • Fat • Happy • Thin • Run • Big • Ugly • Small

104 Go-Togethers

Any (as source of combinations)
Art
English
History & Geography
Maths
PE
PSHE
Science

Objective To quickly think of things that go together.

Props Pencil & paper

- *I am going to say the first part of a phrase you are familiar with: 'fish and ... ' What part have I left out? Shout it out.*
- Here are a few more to practice with:
- *brothers and ...*
- *cats and ...*
- *peaches and ...*
- Pair the group. Make sure each pair has a pencil and paper.
- *You and your partner must quickly think of what's been left off and write it down. See how many you can get.*
- This can be a competition if you like, but it is not necessary. The challenge is inherent.

Individuals
Partners
Small Group
Whole Group

There may be appropriate responses that differ from the ones in parentheses:

Mathematics

- add and (subtract)
- multiply and (divide)
- positive and (negative)
- problem and (solution)
- height and (weight)

General

- peanut butter and (jam)
- pancakes and (syrup)
- jelly and (ice cream)
- bread and (butter)
- mothers and (fathers)
- mums and (dads)
- sisters and (brothers)
- grandmothers and (grandfathers)
- keys and (locks)
- shoes and (socks)
- in and (out)
- up and (down)
- north and (south)
- east and (west)

105 Word Tennis

Objective To 'toss' words rapidly back and forth between partners.

- *Face your partner (or members of your group).*
- *This is a quick-thinking talking game.*
- *I will give you a theme – a big idea – and all the words you say must fit into this theme.*
- *For example, if the theme is Food, then you could say, 'eggs, bread, ice cream ... '*
- *The idea is to say a word as quickly as possible. You can't wait more than three seconds or you are out.*
- *If you repeat a word or say 'ah' or 'um', you are out.*
- Provide a theme and watch the fun.
- As you note several pairs finish (i.e., with one person out) stop the game and provide another theme.
- A good idea is to use an idea from a current topic in another subject, such as 'ecosystems' from Science.
- An alternative is to change 'Tennis' to 'Association'. The group members must say whatever the previous word makes them think of. For example, 'Snow' might lead to 'white', to 'black', to 'witch', and so on. This tends to be a bit more difficult, but equally entertaining and thought-provoking.

Any (as source of theme)
Art
English
History & Geography
Maths
PE
PSHE
Science

Individuals
Partners
Small Group
Whole Group

Showcase An entertaining quick conclusion to this activity is to invite any two group members to face-off and attempt the game with everyone watching.

106 Quick Questions

Any

Art

English

History & Geography

Maths

PE

PSHE

Science

Objective To brainstorm as many questions as possible for a given answer (based on the popular U.S. TV show *Jeopardy*).

Props Pencil & paper

- *I am going to give you a statement that will serve as an answer.*
- *You and your partner have to think up and write down as many questions as you can for that answer, in a very short time.*
- *For example, if the answer is 'The ocean', questions might be 'Where do whales live?' or 'What is a large body of water called?'*
- Provide an answer and signal to start.
- Keep the pace quick and count the number of appropriate questions for each answer.

Individuals

Partners

Small Group

Whole Group

107 Big Word/Small Word

Objective To quickly change small words into bigger words.

Props Pencil & paper

- *Sit facing your partner.*
- *Partner A will say a short word, such as 'cat'.*
- *Partner B has to think of a bigger word that has 'cat' in it, such as 'caterpillar'.*
- *As soon as Partner B has come up with the bigger word, B gives A a small word to change into a big word.*
- *Keep a list of your big and small words as you go.*
- For a simplified version of this game, provide a list of small words and get partners to brainstorm the bigger words within a time limit. If competition is desired, the pair with the most big words wins.

Suggested Small Words

• in	• ring	• call
• at	• see	• able
• or	• eat	• all
• if	• do	• part
• ill	• but	• no
• got	• with	
• dog	• ate	

108 Excuses, Excuses

Any

Art

English

History & Geography

Maths

PE

PSHE

Science

Objective To brainstorm more excuses than your partner in a set length of time.

Props Pencil & paper

- *This is a great game that you will all be very good at!*
- *Sit facing your partner.*
- *When I give the Start signal, you and your partner will brainstorm as many excuses as you can for the situation I will provide.*
- *Jot them down. We'll discuss some of them later.*
- *Be creative. The excuses can be as wild or silly as you want.*

Individuals

Partners

Small Group

Whole Group

Extended Follow Up Invite groups to choose one very unusual excuse (their own or someone else's) and elaborate it into a story, written reflection or letter.

Showcase Display a few of the most creative and humorous excuses.

Suggested Scenarios
- Homework not done
- Late for supper (sport practice, school)
- Telling of a secret
- Lost books (little sister, pet, pencil, money)
- Broken ornament (TV, video game, glasses)
- Black eye (torn clothes, missing tooth)
- Possession of kitten (puppy, new bike, new hat/jacket/shoes)

109 Break-Up

Objective To break large words into as many smaller words as possible.

Props Pencil & paper

- *With your partner, you have to make as many small words as you can from the word I give you.*
- *You can use only the letters from the word as many times as they appear in it. So if the word was 'apple', then you could use two 'p's in the words you make. If the word I give is 'pear', then you have only one 'p' to use.*
- *You will have ten seconds (or up to 60 seconds) to brainstorm and write the new words.*
- *The pair with the most words wins.*
- Use subject-related words to be reinforced: e.g., equilateral, Mesopotamia, equation, geography. These can be written on the board if necessary.

Suggested Words

- multicultural
- extraordinary
- catastrophic
- spaghetti
- pumpernickel

If They Could Talk

Any

Art

English

History & Geography

Maths

PE

PSHE

Science

Objective To think of the things inanimate objects might say, if only they could talk.

Props Pencil & paper

- *Take out a piece of paper and something to write with.*
- *You and you partner are going to use your combined imaginations to brainstorm.*
- *I will give you the name of some inanimate object (something without life) and you will think of all the things that object might say if it were alive.*
- *For example, if I said 'apple', you might write, 'Please don't eat me', or 'I want to be in a pie'.*
- *You will have 60 seconds to think. Then we'll discuss a few of your ideas.*

Individuals

Partners

Small Group

Whole Group

Extended Follow Up Use the brainstormed ideas as story starters or discussion openers.

111 First & Last

Objective To quickly say a word that begins with the last letter of the word spoken by the previous person.

- *For this game, you will need to concentrate on word spellings.*
- *Your job is to think of a word that starts with the last letter of the word you partner says.*
- *For example, if I said 'father', my partner would have to say a word starting with 'r', such as 'right'. Then I'd say a word that starts with 't', and so on.*
- *You have to think and speak as quickly as possible.*
- *This is a competition between you and your partner. If either of you can't think of a word in two seconds, if you repeat a word or if you say 'er' or 'uh', the other person wins.*
- *I will give you the first word.* Signal to start by giving a word.

5 Beyond the Three-Minute Mark

The activities in this section often *stretch* the 3-minute limit and have, therefore, been separated. Although these activities may take longer to execute – sometimes up to ten minutes or more – they still work well as refocusers or motivators, as long as group leaders debrief in such a way as to return the group's focus to the interrupted lesson or activity.

These activities involve the whole group in challenging, enjoyable and intrinsically motivating activities. These ten-minute motivators involve cognition, short-term memory, all manner of communication, listening and viewing. Frequently an element of competition is involved, together with a consistent requirement for cooperation. Often two or more people are 'It'; they may be asked to leave the room for a few moments until the group is ready, then return to engage in a mutually entertaining challenge. Group members generally *want* to be 'It'. Once they realise the activity is fun, they are eager to be the 'main characters'.

- Group leaders should remind everyone of the importance of respect, of 'no wrong responses' and of demonstrating appreciation for individual efforts.
- Naturally, no one should ever be forced to be 'It'; however, it is equally important to encourage everyone to take turns, especially if the same few are always eager to volunteer.

These motivators also make excellent introductory activities for lessons. For this reason, a more detailed list of suggested subjects is provided for most of these activities, suggesting curriculum areas where they may work well.

112 Obstacle Course

Any

Art

English

History & Geography

Maths

PE

PSHE

Science

Objective To lead a 'blind' partner through an obstacle course of people.

- Begin by dividing into two groups. One group (A) will be the obstacles, while the other group (B) takes the Trust Walk. Halfway through the activity, you can reverse the groups.
- *This game involves trust. You will need to really trust your partner.*
- *Group A, I want you to position yourselves any way you want to, as long as your body presents an obstacle in the room. For example, you might spread your arms and legs into an X, or you might sit down and become a 'rock'.*
- *Group B, you will have to get past these obstacles from one side of the room to the other. In pairs, decide who is A and who is B.*
- *Partner A, you are the first follower. This means you must shut your eyes during the game and keep them shut until your partner has led you past the obstacles.*
- *Partner B, you have to carefully lead your partner past the obstacles. You can talk to your partner, guide her or him by the shoulders – whatever you need to do. But you must be responsible; don't let your partner get hurt.*
- Allow both groups to experience being both followers and leaders. You may wish to separate this into two activities, rather than have both groups go through the entire experience at once.

Individuals

Partners (as part of Whole Group)

Small Group

Whole Group

Follow Up Quickly discuss how it felt to be a leader, a follower and an obstacle.

Extended Follow Up Discuss at length various situations in which trust is imperative. This could be extended to a discussion about professions where trust is involved (e.g., police officers).

113 Let's Quiggle

Objective To guess, by asking pertinent questions, what activity the class has secretly selected.

English (grammar, verbs, word choices)

Maths (problem-solving)

Science (importance of using good questioning techniques, especially higher-level thinking questions, when examining data or doing experiments)

- *This is a guessing game.*
- *I need two volunteers to leave the room for about 30 seconds. When they return, they will have to guess what activity, for instance as 'eating', the rest of us have chosen.*
- *The activity will represent an action word, a verb.*
- *The volunteers will ask Yes/No questions substituting the word 'quiggle' for the activity to be guessed.*
- *For example, if they ask, 'Do you quiggle at home?' for 'eating' we would answer, 'Yes'.*
- *If they ask 'Are you quiggling all the time?' we would answer, 'No'.*
- *They will ask questions until they think they can guess the secret word. Then they get three guesses.*
- Discuss briefly, or provide another example (e.g., 'breathing') until the group has the idea. They will note that the secret activity is actually a verb.
- Send the volunteers out of the room. *Okay, we need to think of a good verb or action word that ends in '-ing'.*
- Bring volunteers back in and let the fun begin.
- If they are stuck, use leading questions that start with 'who', 'when', 'where', 'why', 'how'. For example, with the verb 'eating':
- *Who do you quiggle with most often?*
- *When/where/why do you quiggle?*
- *How do you quiggle?* (The response can be a vague 'With difficulty' or as specific as 'By using my mouth and teeth'.)
- Or provide more specific clues, such as *'I like to quiggle when I'm hungry'.*
- The group will quickly get the idea to respond in a more and more revealing manner, so that the volunteers are given more open suggestions. This is a constant work in progress, with learning going on for all.

Individuals

Partners

Small Group

Whole Group

114 Give Me a Clue

English (research skills)

Maths (problem-solving)

PSHE (awareness of individuality, that people are more than 'what you see')

Science (doing experiments, collecting data)

Objective To work out the answers to riddles, using leading clues provided by the teacher.

Note Riddles taken from *Colorful Lateral Thinking Puzzles,* Paul Sloane & Des MacHale, Sterling Publishing, New York.

- Begin by forming into small groups as quickly as possible.
- *As a group, your job will be to work out the answers to some riddles.*
- *I will give you clues.*
- *The first group to find the answer wins (gets a point)*
- Read out a riddle. Give one clue at a time, allowing about 30 seconds group discussion time before giving the next clue. Continue in this manner.
- If no one gets the answer, provide it fairly quickly so as to maintain the momentum of the game. Use as few or as many riddles as is necessary to refocus the group.
- Any riddles can be used by simply providing a series of consistently more revealing clues.

Follow Up Discuss the importance of looking at all details and thinking in different ways.

Extended Follow Up Challenge the group to create their own riddles and clues.

Individuals

Partners

Small Group

Whole Group

Suggested Riddles

1 What is the only day that doesn't end in a *-y*?

Clues:
- It is the day we all look forward to.
- It arrives many times a week.
- Procrastinators love this day.

Answer: Tomorrow

2 What is unusual about the number 40?

Clues:
- This is not a mathematical property.
- 40 is different from any other number.
- It has to do with order.
- It has a lot to do with spelling.
- It has a lot to do with the alphabet.

Answer: 40 is the only number whose letters are in alphabetical order.

115 The Rule Rules!

Objective To work out which rules the group are using when they answer Yes/No questions.

- *For this game, volunteers will guess what rule the rest of the group is using when they answer Yes/No questions. The rule could be something like, 'Every other person must answer No', or 'Everyone in glasses must answer 'Yes'.*
- *Two volunteers will leave the room. While outside, they should each think of two or three simple questions to which responses will be only 'Yes' or 'No'. The questions should be ones that you already know the correct answers to.*
- *For example, you might ask 'Are you sitting down?' You already know everyone is sitting, so when you get a 'No' answer, that will give you a clue to the rule.*
- *The volunteers will ask the same question to several people in sequence and, based on their answers, try to work out the rule.* Demonstrate this with the 'Are you sitting down?' question. First person answers 'Yes', second answers 'No', third answers 'Yes' and so on.
- *Volunteers get three guesses at the rule.*
- *If you think of funny questions, like 'Are you a monkey?' some people may have to answer 'Yes', because they will have to follow the rule.*
- *Volunteers please leave.* While they are outside, the group must decide on a rule.
- Call volunteers back and let them begin. If they are stuck, help them by suggesting a question yourself and quickly asking a number of people so that the rule becomes apparent.
- Initially, you can let volunteers know which of the three forms of rules – sequence, appearance or actions – are being used; once the class is familiar with the game, you can omit this information.

English
(descriptive writing, detailed writing)

History & Geography
(discussions about political themes, rules and constitution, family connections)

Maths
(problem-solving, fractions)

Suggested Rules based on Physical Appearance

• All those wearing blue (jeans, glasses, shoes, shorts) answer No. • All those with curly hair answer Yes. • All those who have on watches answer No. • All those with books on their desks answer Yes.

Suggested Rules based on Actions

Answer honestly and do the following as you answer or before you answer:

- Touch your face
- Cough slightly
- Say 'hmmmm'
- Take a big deep breath
- Lean forward
- Lift one foot off the floor
- Scratch your head
- Put your hands together
- Bite your lip
- Look up at the ceiling

Individuals

Partners

Small Group

Whole Group

116 Back Talk

History & Geography (how information changes as it is passed along)

Maths (the importance of accurate renditions of numerals)

Objective To pass on a design based on tactile impressions put on the group's backs. No talking allowed.

Props Pencil & paper; card or paper with simple photocopied designs.

- Begin by forming smaller groups, standing in rows, each person facing the back of the person in front. The person at the front has a pencil and piece of paper. The person at the back has a photocopied illustration.
- *This is a game like Chinese Whispers, in which you pass on a message. But this time you will pass a picture. No talking.*
- *The person with the picture must draw the first part of the picture on the back of the person in front, using only a finger.*
- *Then that person draws on the back of the next person and so on, until the drawing reaches the front.*
- *The front person draws on their piece of paper what he or she thinks was drawn on their back, then holds up the pencil to show they have finished.*
- *As soon as the back person sees the raised pencil, the next part of the illustration is drawn on the back of the person in front and so on until the entire illustration is reproduced by the person in front.*
- *Remember – no talking. This is not a race; take your time. When everyone has finished we'll see which group is closest to the original drawing.*
- This is an excellent activity for a very differentiated class or where some members do not speak the language very well. For younger or less able groups, you can start with very simple illustrations or shapes, and draw the whole shape at once.

Individuals

Partners

Small Group

Whole Group

Showcase Displaying the finished illustrations is a natural conclusion and can often be quite humorous.

Suggested Designs

- Stick person with some identifying characteristic, such as a briefcase, big hat, or funny hair
- Fish with interesting gills or fins
- Tree with various fruits or flowers on it
- Happy face with unusual eyes, hair, hat, earrings
- Simple animal with some unusual characteristic, such as rabbit with bow, dog with boots.

117 Shake My Hand

Objective To locate other members of the group who have the same number as you.

Props Small paper slips with the numbers 1 to 5 written on them – enough for the whole group.

- If your group is divisible by 5, then each number group will have an equal number, make sure everyone knows how many are in each number group. You will need to tell everyone that some number groups will have fewer members. Since this is a competitive activity, if you don't let the groups know in advance how many members they have, it becomes an unfair challenge.
- *This game will involve shaking hands with each other, but in a rather unusual way.*
- *Each of you will have a secret number.* Hand out the slips of paper, one per person. *Don't show anyone your number. Remember it, then hide the piece of paper. When I give the Start signal, you will walk around the room shaking hands with everyone you meet.*
- *But here's the catch. If you had the number 3, then you must shake everyone's hands three times.* Demonstrate shaking your hand/arm three times.
- *If you had a 1, shake hands only once. So what will happen when a 1 and a 3 meet?*
- Demonstrate with someone so everyone can see the resistance offered by the 1 when the 3 tries to continue shaking.
- *When you have found someone with the same number as you, link arms and continue to find the other members of your group.*
- *When your group has all its members, quickly sit down on the floor. The first group to sit is the winner.*
- This motivator is a good way to form small groups for subsequent activities.
- Another way to play this game is to ask group members to secretly choose a number between 1 and 5 and then find others who have chosen the same number.

Follow Up Ask what it felt like when they found someone else with the same number.

Extended Follow Up Lengthy discussion about finding someone 'just like you' or 'not at all like you', link to the curriculum connection you may have chosen.

Maths (simple counting)

PSHE (ways to meet and greet)

Science (effects of resistance)

Individuals

Partners

Small Group

Whole Group

118 Tell It Like It Is

English (propaganda, bias, elaboration and literary licence in literature)

History & Geography (historical information, political platforms)

Objective To repeat a story several times and note the changes in content.

Props A short story with many details.

- *For this game four or five volunteers will wait outside while I tell someone a story.*
- *One at a time, the volunteers will return, listen to the story, then retell it to the next volunteer, until everyone has heard the story.*
- *The last volunteer to hear it must retell it to the whole group.*
- This same activity can be done in mime form. The group leader or a member of the group mimes an activity (e.g., changing a baby's nappy, changing a tyre, making a cake or pizza, looking for lost keys) and the volunteers mime it to each other.
- The short story can deliberately be left unfinished so that it can be used for story completion either by writing, discussing or illustrating.

Individuals

Partners

Small Group

Whole Group

Follow Up If the story 'morphed' a great deal (which it usually does), discuss the reasons for this. Equally, if it came out almost the same, discuss the reasons for this.

119 Sense or Nonsense?

Objective To determine which of several volunteers is providing the real definition for an unusual and unfamiliar word.

Props Index cards or slips of paper with unusual words, or new unfamiliar vocabulary from core subjects, printed on one side, with a pronunciation guide and definitions on the backs.

- *This is a word guessing game.*
- *Three volunteers will leave the room with a card that has an unusual word on it.*
- *They will decide who will tell the group the real meaning, while the other volunteers will give you false meanings.*
- *You, as a group, will have guess who is telling the truth.*
- *This is a challenge – the volunteers against the rest of the group.*
- *After all three volunteers have given their meanings we will vote on who has given the correct definition.*
- *If the majority of the group guesses the correct definition, the group are the winners.*
- *If the volunteers manage to confuse you, they win.*
- For younger groups, it may be helpful to provide three definitions on the back of the card: one correct and two false ones. Older groups enjoy creating the false definitions themselves; they soon discover that creating a false definition based at least partially on some component of the word serves to confuse.

Follow Up Ask the group what clues the words may have provided to their actual meanings.

Suggested Words

ULULATE ***you-you-late*** (to wail or howl loudly)
EFFLUVIUM ***ef-floo-vee-um*** (an often foul smelling outflow or vapour)
CASTELLATED ***cas-tell-ate-ed*** having turrets or battlements
VINEGARROON ***vin-i-gar-roon*** a large non-venomous scorpion-like arachnid
TRUNCATE ***trun-kate*** to shorten by cutting off

Any subject where new vocabulary is introduced

English (examination of word parts, root words, word origins, plus close examination and interpretation of non-verbal communication and body language)

Individuals

Partners

Small Group

Whole Group

120 It's MY Story!

English (close examination and interpretation of non-verbal communication and body language, fact versus fiction in literature)

History & Geography (discussions about the relevancy of news reports, historical events reports, textbook depictions of history; collecting data for research)

Objective To decide which of the volunteers is the one that a story actually happened to.

- *Three volunteers will leave the room for a few minutes.*
- *While out, they must think of something interesting that actually happened to one of them, but they when they come back in they will each say it happened to them.* It is helpful to give a quick example here; e.g., 'If Tommy had a bad time at the dentist, Meera would say it happened to her and Dan would say it happened to him'.
- To the volunteers: *You will need to have enough information about the actual event so that two of you can 'lie' convincingly. Your job is to fool the class. If the majority of the class chooses the wrong storyteller, you three are the winners.*
- *The group will be allowed to ask each of you questions. You will answer just as if you were the person in the situation. Naturally, for one of you this will be easy; the other two will have to think quickly and try to answer sensibly.*
- While the volunteers are out, prepare the group by telling them to:
- *Watch for non-verbal cues, such as nervous actions.*
- *Ask questions that will give good information.*
- *Ask the same question to more than one volunteer and compare the answers.*
- *See if the volunteers 'trip themselves up' in any way.*
- Bring the volunteers back in and allow about five minutes of group questioning; then vote on who actually had the experience.

Individuals

Partners

Small Group

Whole Group

Follow Up Ask the group what clues may have been given by the volunteers as to whether or not they were telling the truth and how this information may help them when doing research or collecting data.

121 The Expert

Objective To volunteer to become an expert on a silly or unusual skill or profession and be questioned by the group.

Props Index cards or pieces of paper with unusual professions written on them.

- Ask for volunteers. The number will depend on the amount of time you have. A single volunteer can take from two to five minutes.
- Provide index cards for random selection.
- *Please pick a card.*
- *Tell the class what topic you will be an expert in.*
- *Leave the room; you have two minutes to become the expert in whatever was on the card you selected. When you return, we will question you about your new career. You will answer as if you really were that person. You might want to change the way you stand, talk or move, to seem more like an expert.*
- While the volunteers are out of the room, to the group: *Let's think of how we can ask good questions. What sorts of questions might we ask? This is not a guessing game, just a form of entertainment.* Allow the group to suggest a few questions. These will flow easily once the interview has begun.
- Bring the volunteer back in. Be prepared to help with the interview if the group gets bogged down.

English (related to any literary work where the protagonist is an expert)

PSHE (exploring careers)

Science (the importance of establishing credibility when making generalisations, the importance of asking good questions)

Follow Up After each expert, quickly provide positives about his or her ability to represent.

Extended Follow Up Challenge the group to think of more additional unusual experts. Record these for future games. Ask group members to write about an expert of their choice.

Suggested Experts
- Shoemaker for Aladdin
- Toothpick tester
- Artificial-smoke maker for a rock band
- Guitar-string maker
- Toothpaste tube filler
- Fish gutter
- Chocolate-bar taster
- Lemon squeezer

Individuals

Partners

Small Group

Whole Group

And the Action Is ...

English (learning about adverbs, descriptive writing, verb modifiers)

History/ Geography/ Science (good questioning techniques for research)

Objective To guess selected adverbs that are controlling actions performed by group members.

- *This is a game that involves good questioning techniques.*
- *Two volunteers at a time will leave the room.*
- *While outside, they will think of actions to ask the rest of the group to perform.*
- *For example, they might ask someone to stand up or someone else to stretch.*
- *The actions must be the kind that can be easily done.*
- *But here's the catch. When the person* does *the action, he or she will do it according to a describing word – an adverb – that we have chosen in the main group.*
- *It's the volunteers' job to work out what that adverb is.*
- *For example, if the adverb we had chosen was 'slowly', then the person would stretch s-l-o-w-l-y.*
- *The volunteers may ask up to five people to do actions before they have to guess. Then they have three guesses.*

Individuals

Partners

Small Group

Whole Group

Follow Up Discuss what is known about use of adverbs; e.g., most (probably all those chosen) end in *-ly*.

Extended Follow Up Use the adverbs and actions in a writing task.

123 Action Telephone

Objective To pass a message conveyed only through actions and watch how it changes.

Props Action /Verb Cards (optional)

Note No talking allowed.

- *For this game, your group will stand in a line, all facing the same direction.*
- Be sure to provide a space for each group.
- *The person at the back of the line will be given an Action Card or has to think of an activity.*
- *He or she will tap the person in front on the shoulder. That person will turn around and watch as the person acts out the action.*
- *The second-last person will then tap the person in front of him or her and repeat acting out the action and so on until the front person has received the message.*
- *The front person then performs the action for the rest of the group to see.*
- *No talking in this game. It's all done by actions.*
- *When your group is finished, sit down on the floor and wait for instructions.*
- *This is not a speed challenge. It is a game of communication.*
- Instead of using Action Cards, you can write actions on the board for the 'end' people to see. Then quickly erase these cues.

Showcase Invite groups to demonstrate their messages by having the front people show the rest of the group. Discuss how the original message has changed (or not).

Suggested Action Cards

- Changing a tyre
- Changing a baby's nappy
- Making a cake
- Giving someone a shave and a haircut
- Bathing a big shaggy dog
- Eating ice cream (spaghetti, hot soup)

English
(learning about propaganda techniques, storytelling)

History & Geography
(awareness of how history 'changes' with retelling)

Individuals

Partners

Small Group

Whole Group
(working in Small Groups)

Index